Weight Management
for Triathletes

WEIGHT MANAGEMENT FOR TRIATHLETES

WHEN TRAINING IS NOT ENOUGH

Meyer & Meyer Sport

British Library Cataloguing in Publication Data
A catalogue record for this book is available from the British Library
Weight Management for Triathletes
Maidenhead: Meyer & Meyer Sport (UK) Ltd., 2016
ISBN 978-1-78255-089-1
Aachen, Auckland, Beirut, Cairo, Cape Town, Dubai, Hägendorf, Hong Kong,
Indianapolis, Manila, New Delhi, Singapore, Sydney, Tehran, Vienna
Member of the World Sport Publishers' Association (WSPA)

Manufacturing: Print Consult GmbH, Munich
E-Mail: info@m-m-sports.com
www.m-m-sports.com

TABLE OF CONTENTS

PREFACE

If you think that the price for being lean and eating well is misery and deprivation, then it is no wonder you have still not succeeded. No one wants to live that way, and you don't have to.

The volume of research supporting the health benefits of a plant-based, whole food diet is so vast that it cannot be ignored. From a weight management perspective, eating this way is a game-changer. You don't have to count calories anymore. This means, to a great extent, you don't have to manage your hunger anymore. You can eat as much as you want. But is it that easy?

No matter what food plan you choose, there will always be foods that you should limit and avoid. There will be times when you are out with your friends and they pressure you to have "just one bite" of junk food. You will be alone at night and something from the pantry will be calling your name. You will drag yourself home after a big race or a nightmarish workout and be too darn tired to care about sticking to your plan. It is hard to make a big change in your life and even harder to stick with it forever.

The number of times you have to just say no each day, multiplied by the number of days in the rest of your life, makes such a task seem impossible. But if you change the way you feel about food, change your food preferences, and create habits that put you in control of what you eat, making a permanent change is manageable and, at some point, it actually gets easy. This book will help you learn to happily eat fewer calories for the rest of your life. Yes, happily.

Don't get me wrong—it is hard work to change your beliefs about yourself and about what is possible, especially in the beginning. Reaching your goal weight is an important milestone, but it takes years to truly feel comfortable—really comfortable—in your own skin. Along the way you will reap the rewards of looking and feeling better about yourself than you have in a long time. You will race faster, look younger, and feel masterful! All of those positives will build, layer upon layer, certainty and confidence in your ability to keep the weight off. You will learn to defend your lean weight like a tiger protects her cubs. There is no way you will let things get out of hand ever again. When you reach that level of certainty, the transformation will be complete.

This second edition incorporates several of the exercises I have used with my food coaching clients. It fleshes out and modifies the basic structure of a calorie-counting program, leading you through the process of cognitive reshaping and emotional rewiring. It takes lots of practice, but as a triathlete, you are used to that. It is time to train your brain as rigorously as you train your body. Let's get to work.

INTRODUCTION: YOU CAN'T OUTRUN A BAD DIET

Did you become a triathlete in order to lose weight? Maybe you entered a big race hoping that a massive training program would do the trick. Maybe you have tried dozens of 30 day "challenges", commercial weight loss programs and read every diet book on the bestseller list. No doubt you have had some success —yet here you are, with this book in your hand.

Endless training takes a bite out of excess calories but it is not enough to overcome the habitual overeating that got you here in the first place. The now famous editorial appearing in the British Journal of Sports Medicine says it all, "You cannot outrun a bad diet". It is worth reading in it's entirely at: http://bjsm.bmj.com/content/early/2015/05/07/bjsports-2015-094911.full

It is easy to stay overweight for years, even if you train daily. Here is a list of possible reasons why you are not losing weight, even though you are training for triathlons:

> You are underestimating your intake. You are not weighing and measuring and recording everything.

> You are overestimating your calorie needs. You overload rather than reload after training sessions.

➤   You are carrying around old weight, even if you are currently not overeating on a regular basis.

➤   You are eating in restaurants too often. You don't realize how calorie-packed restaurant food usually is.

➤   You are eating to celebrate your last triathlon finish, or to mourn a poor race performance or for other emotional reasons.

➤   Your "diets" are a temporary thing that you go off of when the weight comes off.

➤   You allow stress/vacation/injury/holidays or some other situations to derail you.

➤   You have a notion that it is unfair/oppressive/not normal to eat carefully all the time.

➤   You tend to abandon your diet and the scale if you get discouraged.

➤   You have a low tolerance for hunger. This is one of the easiest things to manage.

➤   You figure you will fail eventually anyway, so why bother working really hard now?

➤   You feel pressured by others to eat the wrong foods and you give in to that feeling on a regular basis.

➤   You don't really want orknow how to make the required changes in your thinking.

➤   Deep down, you are okay with your current weight. If this is the case, you don't need this book.

➤   You lack sufficient motivation (enthusiasm, pain or anger) to make lasting change.

All that calorie-burning exercise and strutting your stuff as a triathlete makes it in some ways, even more difficult to lose weight.

➤   Your physical ideal is probably leaner than the norm (especially since most people are overweight).

➤ You probably take pride in your ability to hang tough and not quit during your workouts. You know how to suffer but you seem to lose all that determination and drive when it comes to food.

➤ You love the athlete in you but you are embarrassed about the overeater.

It is inconceivable that you don't know what foods to avoid and how to lose weight. There are many different ways of eating that will help you lose weight. But the food you choose is not going to change your way of thinking about yourself and your weight. It won't teach you how to stay lean when you are injured, on vacation or during holidays, or when for one reason or another, your athletic life is put on hold.

You need to think long-term right from the start and to spend more time challenging your thoughts and beliefs about food (as this program does) than you spend looking for a miracle.

Don't worry. You can change. This book will show you how.

PART ONE:
GROUNDWORK

CHAPTER 1:
THE TRUTH ABOUT WEIGHT CONTROL

Extremism in pursuit of permanent lifestyle change is no vice.
Moderation in defense of failure to change is no virtue.
–Daniel S. Kirschenbaum, PhD, in *The 9 Truths about Weight Loss*

Losing weight is hard. Keeping it off is even more difficult. Anyone who tells you that it is as simple as eating X, Y, and Z is wrong. Eating is wrapped up in emotion, and it plays a big part in the social fabric of our lives. But it is ultimately something you can control if you decide to. Once you have decided—really decided—to take control, it gets easier.

Following is a quick list of statements that you should accept as truths to prepare you for successful weight loss. As you read through them, decide if you agree with them before moving to the next one. They are not in any particular order. Read the entire list and mark the top 10, the ones that speak to you the most right now. Those are the ones to start with. Write them down and put the list somewhere visible. Read the list every day. If you balk at any of the statements, take the time to work through them in your head, check facts, talk to others, and accept that these really are true statements.

1.   I WILL SUCCEED WHEN I STOP MAKING EXCUSES.
Reasoning: Every time I have started a program and failed to meet my goal, it has been because something got in the way. I got off track due to a circumstance outside of my control, or I lost motivation. The only one who decides what I put into my mouth is

me, regardless of circumstances. I can always say no to poor quality food, I can always eat less than I am offered, and I can always just be hungry for a few hours. Throwing in the towel because my life gets stressful or because eating well is inconvenient is an excuse. As long as I allow circumstances or other people to control what I eat, I will stay overweight. There is no perfect time to lose weight and it is never easy.

2. GETTING BACK ON TRACK RIGHT AWAY AFTER A SETBACK IS CRITICAL TO MY SUCCESS.

Reasoning: No matter how well I plan, things will go wrong, and there will be events outside my control. My motivation will wane at times, and I will give in and overeat. The damage done by eating one particular thing or having a few bad hours is not such a big deal. It only becomes one when I look at it as a failure and I decide to give up and eat more. I can keep those bad patches very short and will learn how to do so. Every time I get back on my plan after a setback, I know I will feel empowered.

3. I MUST LEARN TO HAPPILY CONSUME FEWER CALORIES FOR THE REST OF MY LIFE IN ORDER TO ACHIEVE LIFETIME WEIGHT CONTROL.

Reasoning: I am not willing to suffer and feel deprived for the rest of my life, but I want to lose weight and keep it off. So I have to find a way to be happy and satisfied with a healthy diet that keeps me lean. This is a task I must accomplish on my own by controlling my thoughts and expectations—just like I have to do when I go through long training days and difficult races. I understand that this is a mental game and that I can prevail.

4. EVERY POWERFUL FOOD THOUGHT MAKES IT EASIER FOR ME TO ACHIEVE MY GOAL.

Reasoning: I sometimes feel that I am at the mercy of food, that it calls to me, and that I am under a spell. But food is just food. It has particular smells, tastes, and textures my brain and body respond to, but I have ultimate control over the thoughts I associate with certain foods. I can learn to find less pleasure in certain foods, and I can learn to enjoy other, healthier foods. I need to pay attention to my food thoughts. If I train my food resistance muscles like I train by body, I will get better at it, and weight control will be easier.

5.   If I not am vigilant about what I eat, I will gain weight no matter how much I train.

Reasoning: When I started training for triathlons, I lost some weight, but then the weight loss stopped. I can only train a certain number of hours per day, and sometimes I feel like a slave to this sport! If I trained for huge races all the time, I could lose more weight, but I don't want to do that. I have other interests and obligations in life beyond training. I have come to realize that I have to be careful about what I eat all the time. If I take time off training, if I get injured, if I—heaven forbid—lose interest in racing, I still want to be lean, so I have to focus on the food—not on the training.

6.   THE ONLY DECISION I HAVE TO MAKE IS TO STAY ON MY PLAN AT THIS MOMENT, NO MATTER WHAT.

Reasoning: My decisions in this moment are the only way I can influence my weight in the future. Making deals with myself to stick to the plan later today will deprive me of my power in this instant. I do not have to carry the burden of what to do 5 minutes or 5 hours from now. All I have is right now.

7.   IT IS IMPORTANT TO REWIRE MY THOUGHTS, BELIEFS, AND FEELINGS ABOUT FOOD SO THAT WEIGHT MANAGEMENT STOPS BEING A STRUGGLE.

Reasoning: I have never really tried to direct that energy to changing my thinking about food. I always used up my energy thinking about what and how much to eat. The thinking part always seemed like a waste of valuable time.

My thoughts about food and weight loss seem normal and, therefore, not something I will have to change. But I understand that if I want to eat differently for the rest of my life without feeling deprived, I will have to change the way I think about food. Otherwise, I will feel deprived all the time, and I don't want that.

For a complete cognitive overhaul of your thinking, see The Beck Diet Solution: Train Your Brain to Think Like a Thin Person by Judith S. Beck [Oxmoor House, 2009].

8.   RESTAURANTS, FAST FOOD, AND THE FOOD INDUSTRY ARE INTERESTED IN PROFIT, NOT IN MY HEALTH. THEY CREATE FOODS THAT ARE EXTREMELY TASTY AND ADDICTIVE. I NEED TO EAT LESS OF THOSE FOODS.

Reasoning: Restaurant foods, especially fast foods, are so appealing. I cannot imagine doing without them. I understand that I have stronger reactions to some foods than to others. It makes sense that I would want fatty, sugary, and salty foods because those are the kind of foods that kept my ancestors alive long enough to reproduce, but they are not ideal for long term health. "Listening to my body" is not as important as using my intellect to make good choices.

For more about the food industry that fuels our food addictions, see Salt Sugar Fat: Explore the Dark Side of the All-American Meal, America's Food Addiction, and Why We Get Fat by Alexandra Kastor [A&S Publishing, 2013]; The End of Overeating: Taking Control of the Insatiable American Appetite by David A. Kessler [Rodale Books, 2010]; and articles by Dr. Joel Fuhrman at www.drfuhrman.com.

9.   I AM STILL ON TRACK AS LONG AS I CONTINUE WITH MY PLAN, NO MATTER WHAT THE SCALE SAYS TODAY.

Reasoning: The changes that I am making in my mind are more important to my long-term success than the number on the scale today. Even if I hit a plateau or I retain water, which happens often after a big workout (due to inflammation), eating well is making currently invisible changes to my metabolism and my body composition. I want to develop habits that will eventually get to me to the weight that is healthy, attractive (I like looking lean), and sustainable. Those habits need to be r developed no matter what the scale shows on any given day.

10.   THE SOCIAL MEDIA, COMMERCIALS AND MY FRIENDS AND FAMILY ARE FULL OF MISINFORMATION ABOUT HEALTHY EATING AND WEIGHT LOSS. I MUST FIND MY OWN RELIABLE SOURCES OF INFORMATION AND DEPEND UPON THOSE.

Reasoning: The amount of available information about "healthy eating" and "weight loss" is staggering! It seems like there are new studies published every day saying this is good for you and that is bad, and then the next day those claims are contradicted. I don't really know what to believe.

I understand that companies often fund their own research in order to support their claims about the healthiness of the food they are trying to sell. I am not equipped to analyze every bit of research that is reported in the media. I am not a nutritionist, and I can't possibly evaluate the validity of everything I read. But it makes sense that if I can find a reputable organization or person that does take the time to do this, I can rely on that source of information. If the source is not out to make a profit on their advice, it is even better.

(Nutritionfacts.org is a non-profit organization created by Dr. Micheal Gregor. Dr. Gregor has devoted his career to evaluating nutrition research and summarizing it in a way that it is useful for public consumption. Start with nutritionfacts.org as a source of information for now and keep a critical eye out for valid nutrition information from other sources, such as DrMirkin.com, ForksoverKnives.com, and DrFurhman.com.)

11.   DIETING IS THE SAME AS LIFELONG WEIGHT CONTROL

Reasoning: If I look at dieting as a temporary state, it is something I am either "on" or "off," and when I reach my goal weight, I will eventually be "finished" with it. This notion is precisely why I have never kept the weight off. Instead, I have to understand that my weight-loss program is really about eating to feed a smaller (leaner) version of myself. In time, my body will shrink into the amount I am feeding it. The way I eat to lose the weight is my new way of eating for life. I have to learn the skills and keep applying them for the reST OF MY LIFE IF I WANT TO STAY LEAN.

12.   EATING A HEALTHY DIET IS NOT AS EXTREME AS THE MEDICAL INTERVENTIONS THAT WILL BE REQUIRED IF I CONTINUE TO EAT POORLY AND GET HEART DISEASE OR DIABETES.

Reasoning: The older I get, the more health problems I see in my friends and family. I understand that diet has a tremendous role in promoting health and preventing disease. Yes, we all know about someone who has lived to an old age despite a poor diet, but those are exceptional cases, and it may turn out that those people eventually will get sick. Everyone dies of something, but it makes sense to eat in the healthiest possible way. If I work to develop healthy eating habits and a powerful mental outlook on food, I will be able to be lean, healthy, and happy. I will be doing the best I can to live a long, full life and that is important to me.

13.   CAN CHANGE HOW I FEEL ABOUT FOOD, AND I CAN LEARN TO ENJOY THE TASTE OF HEALTHY FOODS.

Reasoning: Sometimes when I learn about the foods enjoyed by people of other cultures, I am shocked and disgusted. People eat all sorts of unpleasant things. But it makes sense that food preferences are learned. I can learn to enjoy foods that are different than my current diet. By learning to like the taste and texture of healthy foods, I can have it all-keep the weight off, improve my health, and enjoy eating.

14.   I CAN LOSE WEIGHT AND STAY LEAN FOR THE REST OF MY LIFE IF I DECIDE IT IS IMPORTANT ENOUGH.

Reasoning: If I had to lose the weight and keep it off for life in order to be allowed to live, I would lose the weight. But I am not facing this ultimatum. This is something I want for myself, and in order to succeed, I have to decide over and over and over again that eating the right thing (and thinking the right way about food) in this moment is more important than anything else. I can look upon healthy eating as a life or death decision if I choose to. Every bit of junk food brings death closer; every vegetable extends the length and the joy of my existence. I have to make my food choices this important because no one else will.

15.   MOST OF THE PEOPLE AROUND ME ARE OVERWEIGHT, SO IF I EAT LIKE THEY DO, I WILL BE OVERWEIGHT LIKE THEY ARE.

Reasoning: I want to be leaner than most of my non-triathlete family and friends. Although I want to fit in and participate with family and friends I will have to break from the pack and do things differently if I want a different result. They might notice if I eat differently, they might even pressure me to give up, but eventually they will come to accept that I eat this way.

16. IT WILL TAKE EFFORT TO LEARN TO PREPARE HEALTHIER FOOD. THESE SKILLS ARE IMPORTANT TO MY SUCCESS, BUT I CAN LEARN THEM GRADUALLY.

Reasoning: It would be nice to have a full-time chef that planned all the meals, did the shopping, cooked, and did the dishes afterward, but I don't have that luxury. I will have to learn some new recipes and cooking methods, but I can do it a little at a time. Most people only eat a few things again and again, so I all I need are a few dishes to start with. I can start with breakfast and go from there, adding as needed so I am not overwhelmed by the task.

There are hundreds of plant-based cookbooks and recipes available. A good place to start is The Forks Over Knives Plan: How to Transition to the Life-Saving, Whole-Food, Plant-Based Diet by Alona Puldem, M.D., and Matthew Lederman, M.D., [Touchstone, 2014].

17. IF I EAT MOSTLY LOW-CALORIE DENSITY FOOD, I WILL BE ABLE TO EAT A LOT, AND I WILL NOT HAVE TO BE HUNGRY.

Reasoning: If I eat low-calorie foods, I will be able to eat more food more often. Naturally low-calorie density food, such as fruits, vegetables, and whole grains, is also very nutritious. Indeed, if my diet consisted mostly of low-calorie density foods for the rest of my life, I would not have to count calories, and I would be able to keep weight off even when my training is temporarily sidelined.

18. MY WEIGHT-LOSS PAST DOES NOT DETERMINE MY WEIGHT-LOSS FUTURE.

Reasoning: Sometimes it feels like I am just spinning my wheels, trying to lose weight again and again with the sneaking suspicion that it is hopeless. It is so discouraging, and whenever I try to lose weight, I always get that same bad feeling when I fail. But those accumulated experiences have taught me things. There are all sorts of insights that I have gained, even if I can't list them all right now. Those experiences planted the seeds for what I am undertaking right now. I can use what I have learned, add to that, and solve my weight management problem.

19. I BELIEVE THAT I WILL BE HAPPIER IF I AM LEANER.

Reasoning: It seems morally wrong to judge someone based on their weight, but it happens in my mind anyway. I judge myself harshly as well. I feel that my weight is within my power to control and that I must be leaner in order to be happy and satisfied with my life.

20. I WILL HIT PLATEAUS THAT LAST A LONG TIME, BUT IT DOESN'T MATTER. WITH PERSISTENCE I WILL REACH MY GOAL.

Reasoning: I really want to lose this weight as soon as possible, but it will take as long as it takes. The distress I feel about my weight is the worst when I am either ignoring my weight problems or not seeing results. As long as am eating in a way that weight loss should occur, I feel better, and I know that eventually my body will adapt and get leaner. All I can do is eat as well as possible and accept the rate of weight loss that results.

Which of these truths speak loudest to you? Remember them.

CHAPTER 2:
THE PROGRAM

"And I realized that there's a big difference between deciding to leave and knowing where to go."

–Robyn Schneider

Eating less than you use is a simple concept. Figuring out how to do it day after day without starving yourself as your motivation waxes and wanes is really hard. If you tend to be overweight, you are fighting biology, and that biology stays with you even after you have reached your goal. You will have to deal with your weight forever. So let's get started.

I had to give this program a catchy name that you would remember, so I am calling it the Saint on the Couch, Sinner on the Bike Program. It is laid out in a nutshell in Fig. 1.

Fig.1 Saint on the couch, sinner on the bike weight-loss program

1. Eat a baseline number of calories.
    a. Fruits and vegetables are free calories.
    b. Fuels consumed during training sessions according to guidelines are free calories.
    c. Recovery meals (eaten according to guidelines) are free calories.

2. Follow the rules and apply the tools.
    a. Change what you eat by gradually replacing current foods with plant-based foods.
    b. Change how you think.
    c. Train at lifetime maintenance level.

3. Gradually reduce structure after you reach your goal weight.

BASELINE CALORIES

The calorie baseline is the number of calories used by your body when you are doing your normal daily activities—going to work or school, dealing with your family and social life, and sleeping. It does not include calories burned during training sessions. Wait. Stop there: Why does it not include training which can be such a big calorie burner? Good question.

Don't worry, you will get enough calories to train and recover, but those are treated separately. They are not part of your baseline, and this is why: The amount of training you do from day to day varies. Sometimes you are training for a sprint race, other times a marathon, and sometimes even an Ironman. You train in different phases; sometimes you taper and do very little. There are also weeks when you are unable to train. You get injured. You get busy. You will get motivated, and you will get burned out. By teaching yourself to eat the same number of calories (more or less) all the time for breakfast lunch and dinner, you will create habits that will keep you lean no matter what your training status is.

You will learn how to set your baseline calories later in this book. In order to keep from feeling deprived and hungry, you will have to modify your existing diet to provide greater food volume. It is no coincidence that high-volume foods tend to be nutritious, plant-based foods. And it is also no coincidence that other than a few exceptions (white potatoes, avocados, and bananas), the high-volume foods have so few calories that you don't even have to count them against your calorie totals. So you could theoretically eat fruits and vegetables all day to the point that you are stuffed, and none of those calories count.

The longer you keep the weight off, the larger your vocabulary of low-calorie foods becomes. This is one of the ways that maintaining your weight will become easier. And yes, you can follow this program and still eat whatever you want as long as you count the calories.

It would be nice and streamlined to change both your calorie intake and your food preferences at the same time. This program certainly gives you lots of information about how to do that, but you can absolutely succeed without changing any of the foods you currently eat. It is emotionally difficult to change your eating habits, and right now, the focus needs to be on weight loss. You can improve diet quality at your own pace. For now, it is all about tracking (i.e., weighing, measuring, and recording) all of those calories not from fruits and vegetables against your baseline.

Fig 2: Tracking supplies

You will need:

➤ Measuring cups

➤ Measuring spoons

➤ A food scale that reads both ounces and grams

➤ A way to record your food intake no matter where you are

Fruits and Vegetables are Free Calories

Fruits and vegetables do have calories, but they aren't counted because these foods are so high in nutritional value and so relatively low in calories that it is unlikely that you will binge on them. They will fill you up, and you will end up eating fewer high-calorie foods in the long run.

Training Fuels are Free Calories

Foods ingested during training sessions are also free calories. These typically include gels and energy drinks and bars, but they can also include candy, sandwiches, and salty snacks. Truly, anything you eat while you are exercising is not counted against your baseline calories. Does that mean you could stop and pick up an entire pizza and it is OK as long as you eat it while you are sitting on your bike? No. The foods that are free are the things you would actually eat when you are doing a real workout. The amount of fuel you take in should be in line with the guidelines set later in this book. As long as you are taking in around 200 calories per hour according to those guidelines, the calories are free. The only counting you need to do is at the beginning of the workout to make sure you have enough calories on board.

Sugary food is convenient, widely available, and necessary for your workouts. The body processes sugar differently when you are exercising, so it is not nearly as damaging as when consumed while at rest. Sugar is also something we crave, so being able to eat it during your workouts is a way to satisfy your sweet tooth and feel less deprived. It is an all-around win.

These calories are free because athletes rarely overeat during training sessions. It is much more common to struggle with getting enough calories into your mouth while you exercise.

It is also a hassle to weigh and measure calories in versus calories out during workouts. It is easy to start out with a 300-calorie bottle of liquid fuel, but what if you don't drink the entire bottle on the ride? Do you want to have to pour the remainder out of your sticky bottle and measure it so you know the calories to subtract? Likewise, candy and gels get discarded, wet, fall apart, or lose their appeal. It is tedious to have to be precise about what you did or didn't eat in a given workout, especially when you are counting every morsel you eat the rest of the time. There is a limit to how much data a person wants to deal with.

That said, the topic of what and how much and when to eat during workouts is very important from a performance standpoint. I encourage you to experiment with various fuels and to find what will work for you, but these considerations need not be part of your weight management program. When you are losing weight, focus on losing weight. That is what is most important right now.

Recovery meals (eaten according to guidelines) are free calories

Recovery meals are to be eaten soon after your longer workouts using the Simple 100 rule (discussed shortly). The guideline frees you from the chore of calculating the precise number of calories expended in a workout. Those calculations (even the ones that show on your fitness device) are usually wrong, and they lead to overeating and, thus, slowing or halting your weight loss. Start with the guideline amounts and adjust as needed, depending on whether you are losing too much weight or not enough.

These separate rules for training-related eating make it easy to eat more on big training days when you need it most. They teach you to look at training as separate from the activities of daily life and daily eating. Blurring those lines has gotten you into the habit of overeating in the past, so this program will bring them back into view.

FOLLOW THE RULES AND USE THE TOOLS

    a.   Change what you eat
    b.   Gradually replace current foods with plant-based foods
    c.   Change how you think
    d.   Train at maintenance level

The mechanics of eating fewer calories are complex. There is more to it than simply choosing lower calorie foods. By structuring your life in such a way that you can establish important new habits, the process of losing weight will be much easier. Later chapters will describe how to change what you eat, how to replace current food with plant-based foods, and how to think about food.

If you can, keep your training load within 6 to 8 hours per week as you use this plan. Your focus should be on eating less, not on training more. The 6 to 8 hours of training per week is the amount of daily exercise that successful weight-loss maintainers sustain year after year. Think of an hour a day of exercise as the bare minimum that you will need for the rest of your life.

GRADUALLY REDUCE STRUCTURE

This is a long-term plan. It will take more than a year to work through the entire program. As you pass through each phase, the level of structure, as well as effort you need to expend, will be reduced.

We all understand the difference between the first few days of a weight-loss plan and "normal" eating. When you start a new diet, you follow strict rules and direct a lot of energy toward food planning, preparing, and calculating. Rules tend to be black or white. When you are following the rules, you are on your plan. When you stop following the rules, you are off your plan, and the weight returns.

The problem with most diet rules is twofold:

1. The rules aren't particularly helpful or meaningful. They don't teach you anything.
2. The rules don't apply once the weight is gone.

The rules and tools in this program are all meaningful and helpful, but they aren't exhaustive. This is very much a personal journey, so I encourage you to develop some of your own. Read the ones in this book and practice them as you lose weight. It might be tempting, but don't dismiss any of them until you have reached your goal weight and maintained it for six weeks. By then you will know which ones to hold on to. You will have assimilated many of them, and maintaining your weight will be pretty simple.

Vigilance is Key

The most critical skill to maintain for lifetime weight control is vigilance. By the time you have lost all the weight, you will be sensitive to behavior that can lead to overeating. You must remain sensitive to this and act upon it quickly—even after you have been lean for five years! Recognizing bad behavior and acting on it immediately is the only way to keep the weight off.

This means that 3 years from now at your birthday party, you will still refuse to bring the leftovers home because you know that cake will end up in only one place—in and then on your body.

This means that you will never "throw in the towel" for days or weeks and gorge yourself when you are emotionally traumatized.

This means that day after day, every time you are in the grocery store, you will take pause before you buy food that is likely to engage you in a battle of wills.

This means that as soon as your wetsuit feels more snug than usual-you will take action.

As of now, the blinders are coming off and going in the garbage.

PART TWO:
THE BODY

CHAPTER 3:
BODY COMPOSITION

It's simple, if it jiggles, it is fat.

—Arnold Schwarzenegger

Leaner Is Faster

There is no set standard of body fat for any sport. It is not the rules, but the demands of the sport that dictate the body-fat levels of high-performing athletes. Consider this:

> The body-fat percentages reported in triathletes by the United States Olympic Committee are 10 to 23% for females, 3 to 9% for males.

> In a 2009 study, triple-Ironman athletes were analyzed for body-fat percentage, training volume, and various body dimensions to determine which characteristics were associated with the fastest finish times. Low body fat was the best predictor of a fast race time. It was more important than any other measurement of body size. It was even more important than training volume (Knechtle et al., 2009).

> Numerous body parameters of elite and junior elite triathletes were measured at the 1987 World Triathlon Championships. Of the components tested, body-fat level was the best predictor of an athlete's success (Landers et al., 2000).

People that tend to carry weight face an enormous challenge if they want to achieve the body-fat levels of a competitive triathlete. But most age-groupers are focused more on improving their own performance, and getting leaner is a powerful tool for doing so.

It is helpful to know your current body composition because this will help you set a goal weight, but it is not required.

Body Build

The three components of body build are frame size, body type, and body composition. Each component of body build has a role in your potential as an athlete and in your appearance.

You can't change the size of your skeleton (i.e., frame size). Body type can't be changed either, but understanding the various types will help you formulate a realistic goal (see fig. 3).

Body composition is where the action is. Training and diet can profoundly influence the ratio of lean mass to fat mass in any body type.

Fig. 3 Summary of body types

Body Type

There are three body types but no one is only one type. We are all combinations of the three. The process of determining body type is known as somatotyping. The brawny football players that populate the Clydesdale divisions have predominantly endomorphic characteristics and pro triathletes are mostly ectomorphs. No amount of training or diet manipulation will transform one body type into another. The best you can do is become a lean, strong, and fit version of yourself.

Endomorph

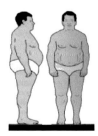

- ⬥ Stocky, pear-shaped body, short arms and legs
- ⬥ Wide hips and shoulders
- ⬥ Wider front to back rather than side to side
- ⬥ A lot of fat on the body, upper arms, and thighs
- ⬥ Gains muscle and fat easily
- ⬥ Has hard time with agility, speed, and sustained running but has high lung capacity

Mesomorph

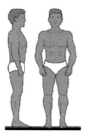

- ◊   A wedge-shaped body
- ◊   Wide, broad shoulders and narrow hips
- ◊   Muscled arms and legs
- ◊   Narrow from front to back rather than side to side
- ◊   Minimum amount of fat, can lose weight easily
- ◊   Excels in strength, agility, and speed sports

Ectomorph

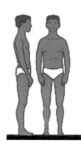

- ◊   Receding chin
- ◊   Narrow shoulders and hips
- ◊   A narrow chest and abdomen
- ◊   Thin arms and legs
- ◊   Little muscle and fat, easily gets lean and hard-looking
- ◊   Excels at endurance sports and gymnastics
- ◊   Superior thermoregulation

*Illustrations reprinted with permission from Brian Mac, www.brianmac.co.uk.

BODY COMPOSITION

What Is Lean Mass?

You hear the terms body fat, BMI, and lean mass thrown around, but do you know what they mean? Body fat is pretty clear; it is the number of pounds of fat on your body, usually expressed as a percentage of total body weight. Triathletes want the body-fat number to be low because extra fat is metabolically inactive tissue that does not contribute to performance; it just has to be carried around. Carrying extra fat is a real disadvantage in running and uphill cycling, both activities that require the athlete to tangle with gravity.

Lean mass is more interesting. Lean mass is everything other than fat. It is not just muscle. Lean mass is also your organs and your skeleton. Your bones account for about 14% of total body weight (Reynolds and Karlotski, 1977). What you may not realize is that stomach contents and even water are counted as lean mass. That is why it is important to get tested under the same circumstances each time. If you get tested after a meal, the numbers will be different than after an overnight fast. A training session can dehydrate you a little, which will also influence results. Drinking a big glass of water before testing does more than increase your weight a few ounces; the water will be counted as lean mass. The differences do not reflect changes in the amount of muscle you have, but rather the other components of lean body mass.

BMI was developed as a tool to identify patients at risk for particular health conditions. Although it doesn't tell an athlete much about the composition of the body, some coaches use a rule of thumb that an athlete will be most competitive at his or her safe lowest BMI. It is discussed at the end of the chapter.

Stick With One Method

It is important to choose a method of body composition analysis, a device, or a particular testing facility that you can stick with for a few years. If you jump around, there will be a lot of variation in your data, and it will be harder to see progress. There is a margin of error in every type of analysis, but it is smaller in some methods than in others. Pick an accurate method.

If losing fat is important to you, take care to get helpful results. Helpful results will show how and if your body composition has changed. You can't gauge this properly if you compare results of a skinfold with results from a handheld device. Athletes who do this have no way of knowing which results are accurate and, more importantly, they can't tell if their fat-loss efforts have been effective. Getting a surprisingly high body-fat reading from a portable device at a race expo can ruin your day and your race if you take it too seriously. Why put yourself through that?

Persevere with one method until you reach your goal.

MEASURING METHODS

Digital Imaging

Computer applications that measure various dimensions of the body with digital imaging are flooding the market, mostly for the purpose of fitting clothing as an alternative to measuring tapes. One company, Lean ScanTM, is in the process of patenting an application that takes this body measurement a step further into the realm of estimating body mass and BMI. This technology will continue to improve by leaps and bounds in years to come.

Bioimpedance Devices

One of most common and widely available methods for measuring body fat is with bioimpedance devices. These devices include portable handheld versions, special bathroom scales, and machines that are used in a clinical setting, such as a doctor's office.

Handheld Devices

Handheld devices pass an electric current from one hand through the body to the other hand. Health clubs and race expos often use these devices because they are portable and easy to use (Varady et al., 2007).

Measurements from these devices are not very accurate. They tend to underestimate lean body mass by 2.3 to 5.6 kg (5.06-12.32 lb) and to underestimate fat mass even more (Varady et al., 2007).

These devices are not a good way to determine how much of your body weight is lean mass and how much is fat. You can compare readings over time to see if there is a trend in one direction or another.

Home Scales

Home body-fat scales measure electrical current from one foot to the other, but they lack input from the torso. The computer inside the scale uses a formula to estimate the torso numbers then combines them with the measurement from the lower body to determine the result displayed on the scale. Studies have compared results with people of different body shapes using these scales. The scales are fairly accurate in women with a pear-shaped body, but the accuracy is very poor in women with an apple-shaped body and for men (Swan and McConnell, 1999).

The company Tanita has overcome this issue by adding handles to some models. The user can measure the composition of the upper body by using the handles and the lower-body composition by standing on the scale and using the foot sensors. Users can even measure composition of each limb, which can be important when trying to overcome an injury or strength or mass imbalance between limbs.

Body water is also displayed on some scales. Body water is simply hydration. An athlete should be able to tell the difference between dehydration and fat loss with one of these scales.

Testing In a Clinic

When testing is done in a doctor's office using bioimpedance, the athlete lies down, and electrodes are placed on a hand and foot. A current is then passed through the entire body. One of the main advantages of this method is that the testing is done by trained personnel under standard conditions (Varady et al., 2007). When done this way, the results are quite accurate.

Displacement Methods

The Bod Pod

Measuring body composition by air displacement plethysmography has become popular with the introduction of the BOD POD® Body Composition Tracking System (see fig. 4). It has taken some time, but since its introduction in 1994, this device has become widely available in athletic testing and training facilities, gyms, and even some health food stores.

The BOD POD® measures the volume of the athlete's body as he sits in a small fiberglass chamber. The body's volume is the amount of air displaced by the athlete when he gets into the chamber. By breathing into an air circuit, the amount of air in the lungs is subtracted and true body volume is calculated.

This method provides consistent readings, but it tends to underreport absolute percentages of body fat (Collins et al., 1999). One of the advantages of this method is that it requires little of the technician doing the measuring so repeated measures over time are likely to be consistent.

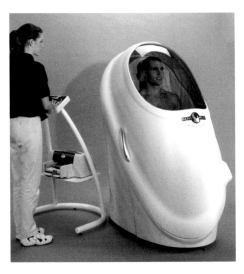

Fig. 4 The Bod Pod

Hydrostatic Weighing

Hydrostatic weighing, also known as underwater weighing, works by comparing dryland weight with the weight while submerged in a tank of water. Body density is estimated from the difference of the two weights, and then a formula is used to calculate the amount of body fat and, thus, body-fat percentage.

This method is highly accurate but not particularly convenient. It is time consuming and requires a large specialized tank. Subjects must get wet and hold their breath for 10 to 20 seconds.

Skinfold Analysis

Skinfold measurement is among the most accurate methods of assessing body composition. It is well worth the embarrassment of having someone grab and measure your fat.

This method uses various formulas and tables which are based upon the number and location of skinfolds tested. Testing can be done at three, four, or seven locations. The measurements are based upon the relationship between subcutaneous fat, which is under your skin, and visceral fat, which is internal, between your organs.

Skinfold testing should be done by a trained clinician. The skin should be measured within two seconds of pinching, and, ideally, measurements should be taken by the same person each time you are tested. In any case, returning to the same facility makes it more likely that the technicians have been trained to follow the same protocol.

This method has had some accuracy problems in the past because the formulas to convert skinfold measurements into body-fat percentages did not work very well in Hispanic and African American men and women; they require different conversion formulas because of differences in body structure (Heyward, 1996; Jackson et al., 2009).

The New Zealand Triathlon Academy uses the skinfolds only without applying any formulas. This method does not give body composition percentages, but it accounts for changes up or down. Current criteria for the sum of eight skinfolds for the academy triathletes are 35 to 75 mm for males and 45 to 100 mm for females (Hellemans, 1999).

Do It Yourself?

Home calipers are widely available and are useful for triathletes who want to see if they are getting leaner or not. They have some advantages over a bioimpedance device in that they do not require batteries and do not involve electronics that may be sensitive to floor surfaces and moisture. Up to four skinfold sites can be used. The measurements can be compared to a chart or used in an online calculator to estimate body-fat percentage, but the results are not very accurate.

Imaging Technologies

X-rays and MRIs can be used to measure the size and location of fatty tissue as well as estimate bone density and lean body mass. These technologies are expensive and time consuming and at this point, not used much for athletes interested in body composition analysis. They are extremely accurate.

FACTORS THAT INFLUENCE RESULTS

Many factors can influence body composition results. Check with the facility beforehand to find out what to wear and how to best time eating, drinking, and training to optimize results. Write the protocol down so you can repeat it precisely each time you are tested. Here is a list of some of the things that can influence results (Jeukendrup and Gleeson, 2004; Le Carvennec et al., 2007; Fields et al., 2004):

1. Hydration status; liquids and alcohol consumed within 24 hours of testing
2. Dampness or sweat on skin
3. Body temperature
4. Time since your last training session
5. Ethnicity
6. Gender
7. Age
8. Level of adiposity
9. Competence of person performing the test
10. Reliability of the computer model and formulas used to calculate results
11. Medications in your system that influence hydration or inflammation

How to Use the Results

Body composition information is most important when you are setting goals or want to see how your body has responded to a particular training or diet regimen.

When you have your body composition analyzed, get as much data as you can from the technician. Sometimes you are given only the body fat %. Ideally, you will receive a written report with all sorts of data such as total lean body mass, total fat body mass, total body weight and if applicable, skinfold measurements.

Use Your Home Scale

Weigh yourself at home as soon as you are done with your body composition test. Compare your weight on your home scale with the one at the testing center and make a note if there is a difference. Now you know how much you weigh at a given percentage of body fat, and you can use the scale to follow your weight-loss progress. Have your body composition retested at least every six months.

The Body Check

Can you imagine there was a time when the only method commonly used to evaluate body fat was the good ol' eyeball? Even in this age of advanced technology, the eyes are among the finest instruments. The only problem is that you can't see your backside very well.

Once you reach your goal, spend some time looking at yourself. You will look so darn good it will be a pleasure, but that is not why you are looking. Take in the details. Create a new vision of "normal" in your mind. Notice the striations on that muscle when you are lean? When you sit down, pull up your shirt and study your belly; what do you see? Memorize the details. In the future you can use your eyes to tell you are putting on fat.

Limitations of the Body Mass Index

The body mass index (BMI) was designed as a simple tool to help evaluate an individual's risk for particular diseases such as stroke, hypertension, and certain cancers. The BMI does not tell you much about how you are built or what proportion of your body weight is lean mass (bone, muscle, organs) and what proportion is fat. Two individuals may have identical BMI numbers but vastly different body-fat levels. Figure 5 illustrates this point. Charts and online calculators are widely available, and they make it simple to determine your BMI. All you need to know is your height and weight.

Weight management programs use BMI as a basis for determining goal weights for clients, but the BMI doesn't give triathletes what they need to know in order to improve body composition.

Fig. 5 Comparison of body composition measures of two men with same BMI

Subjects	BMI	Body fat (%)	Total fat weight (pounds)	Total lean weight (pounds)
Tom: 5'0" 128 pounds	25	6.25	8	120
Joe: 6'0" 186 pounds	25	4.0	26	160

The athletes in figure 5 illustrate the limitations of BMI as a measure of body composition. While both athletes are in the healthy weight range, there is a large difference between their body-fat levels.

Although BMI is not a way to determine body fat, it can be a starting point for weight loss. Endurance athletes are likely to fall in the bottom half of the BMI range for a given height.

PART THREE:
PLANNING

CHAPTER 4:
MAKE A PLAN

Never, Never, Never, Never Give Up

Your weight management plan will have several phases—similar to having training phases to prepare for your races. The difference is that your training plan has a specific end date race day. Your weight-loss plan will be based only on estimates. Each phase will be described in detail in a later section. The first thing you have to do to set up your plan is to establish your starting point and where you want to go from there.

Fig. 6 Setting up your weight-loss program with basic information

Weight-Loss Phase						
	Goal weight:					
	Goal BMI/Body composition:					
	Starting weight:					
	Starting BMI/Body comp:					
	Estimated duration of weight-loss phase:					
	Baseline calories:					
	Victory race dates:					

START WITH YOUR GOALS

There are lots of things to consider as you decide on a weight goal.

➤ The goal has to be motivating. The thought of achieving it should be exciting. It should be something that would change how you view yourself. It should put you into a different category of fitness and performance, or at least you should look like you are faster and fitter than ever.

➤ It has to be attainable. In other words, it has to match all the things you cannot change: your height, bone structure, body build, and your age.

Body Mass Index (BMI) Table for Adults

Obese (>30) · Overweight (25-30) · Normal (18.5-25) · Underweight (<18.5)

HEIGHT in feet/inches and centimeters

WEIGHT lbs (kg)	4'8" 142cm	4'9" 147	4'10" 150	4'11" 152	5'0" 155	5'1" 157	5'2" 160	5'3" 163	5'4" 165	5'5" 168	5'6" 170	5'7" 173	5'8" 175	5'9" 178	5'10" 180	5'11" 183	6'0" 185	6'1" 188	6'2" 191	6'3" 193	6'4"	6'5" 196
260 (117.9)	58	56	54	53	51	49	48	46	45	43	42	41	40	38	37	36	35	34	33	32	32	31
255 (115.7)	57	55	53	51	50	48	47	45	44	42	41	40	39	38	37	36	35	34	33	32	31	30
250 (113.4)	56	54	52	50	49	47	46	44	43	42	40	39	38	37	36	35	34	33	32	31	30	30
245 (111.1)	55	53	51	49	48	46	45	43	42	41	40	38	37	36	35	34	33	32	31	31	30	29
240 (108.9)	54	52	50	48	47	45	44	43	41	40	39	38	36	35	34	33	33	32	31	30	29	28
235 (106.6)	53	51	49	47	46	44	43	42	40	39	38	37	36	35	34	33	32	31	30	29	29	28
230 (104.3)	52	50	48	46	45	43	42	41	39	38	37	36	35	34	33	32	31	30	30	29	28	27
225 (102.1)	50	49	47	45	44	43	41	40	39	37	36	35	34	33	32	31	31	30	29	28	27	27
220 (99.8)	49	48	46	44	43	42	40	39	38	37	36	34	33	32	32	31	30	29	28	27	27	26
215 (97.5)	48	47	45	43	42	41	39	38	37	36	35	34	33	32	31	30	29	28	28	27	26	25
210 (95.3)	47	45	44	42	41	40	38	37	36	35	34	33	32	31	30	29	28	28	27	26	26	25
205 (93.0)	46	44	43	41	40	39	37	36	35	34	33	32	31	30	29	29	28	27	26	26	25	24
200 (90.7)	45	43	42	40	39	38	37	35	34	33	32	31	30	30	29	28	27	26	26	25	24	24
195 (88.5)	44	42	41	39	38	37	36	35	33	32	31	31	30	29	28	27	26	26	25	24	24	23
190 (86.2)	43	41	40	38	37	36	35	34	33	32	31	30	29	28	27	26	26	25	24	24	23	23
185 (83.9)	41	40	39	37	36	35	34	33	32	31	30	29	28	27	27	26	25	24	24	23	23	22
180 (81.6)	40	39	38	36	35	34	33	32	31	30	29	28	27	27	26	25	24	24	23	22	22	21
175 (79.4)	39	38	37	35	34	33	32	31	30	29	28	27	27	26	25	24	24	23	22	22	21	21
170 (77.1)	38	37	36	34	33	32	31	30	29	28	27	27	26	25	24	24	23	22	22	21	21	20
165 (74.8)	37	36	34	33	32	31	30	29	28	27	27	26	25	24	24	23	22	22	21	21	20	20
160 (72.6)	36	35	33	32	31	30	29	28	27	27	26	25	24	24	23	22	22	21	21	20	19	19
155 (70.3)	35	34	32	31	30	29	28	27	27	26	25	24	24	23	22	22	21	20	20	19	19	18
150 (68.0)	34	32	31	30	29	28	27	27	26	25	24	23	23	22	22	21	20	20	19	19	18	18
145 (65.8)	33	31	30	29	28	27	27	26	25	24	23	23	22	21	21	20	20	19	19	18	18	17
140 (63.5)	31	30	29	28	27	26	26	25	24	23	23	22	21	21	20	20	19	18	18	17	17	17
135 (61.2)	30	29	28	27	26	26	25	24	23	22	22	21	21	20	19	19	18	18	17	17	16	16
130 (59.0)	29	28	27	26	25	25	24	23	22	22	21	20	20	19	19	18	17	17	16	16	16	15
125 (56.7)	28	27	26	25	24	24	23	22	21	21	20	20	19	18	18	17	17	16	16	16	15	15
120 (54.4)	27	26	25	24	23	23	22	21	21	20	19	19	18	18	17	17	16	16	15	15	15	14
115 (52.2)	26	25	24	23	22	22	21	20	20	19	19	18	17	17	16	16	15	15	14	14	14	14
110 (49.9)	25	24	23	22	21	21	20	19	19	18	18	17	17	16	16	15	15	15	14	14	13	13
105 (47.6)	24	23	22	21	21	20	19	19	18	17	17	16	16	16	15	15	14	14	13	13	13	12
100 (45.4)	22	22	21	20	20	19	18	18	17	17	16	16	15	15	14	14	14	13	13	12	12	12
95 (43.1)	21	21	20	19	19	18	17	17	16	16	16	15	15	14	14	13	13	13	12	12	12	11
90 (40.8)	20	19	19	18	18	17	16	16	15	15	15	14	14	13	13	13	12	12	12	11	11	11
85 (38.6)	19	18	18	17	17	16	16	15	15	14	14	13	13	13	12	12	12	11	11	11	10	10
80 (36.3)	18	17	17	16	16	15	15	14	14	13	13	13	12	12	11	11	11	11	10	10	10	9

Fig. 7 Using BMI as a shortcut to setting goals

Consider What Is Ideal for the Sport

Triathletes strive for a combination of three body type ideals: swimming necessitates buoyancy (requiring some body fat), runners desire no excess weight, and cyclists strive for strength and stamina. If optimal performance is driving your quest for leanness, it is likely that leaner is better, within reason. Consider the body-fat percentages of high-level triathletes as set forth in figure 8.

Fig. 8 Body-fat percentage of high-level athletes

Body-fat percentage	Female range (%)	Male range (%)
Swimming	14-24	7-12
Cycling	12-18	8-10
Running	10-19	6-13
Triathlon	10-23	3-9

The body-fat values in figure 8 are given as a range because individuals vary. Not every male athlete will achieve his best performance at 8% body fat. Some will reach lower values and still improve performance, while others will find it impossible to get down that low and will have to compete at a higher value. Women should not strive for single-digit body-fat levels because they are unhealthy.

Do you know how your own performances vary with body composition or weight? Some athletes have kept track of this information throughout several training seasons . Those are the ones who aren't reading this chapter because they already know what their goals are. By tracking your own race performances you will discover what is optimal.

CONSIDER WHO YOU ARE

Don't Look Too Far Back

As long as we are talking about history, it may be tempting to use your weight in high school or at some other time when you were fit and healthy as your goal. That number may be emotionally powerful for you, but consider carefully whether it is right for you now.

> You probably have tried to get back to that number many times in your life, so it is connected with past failures. Does that more strongly compel you to reach it, or does it open a troubling can of worms? Maybe a new number a few pounds heavier would be better.

> Were you a triathlete back then? Your goal should reflect your identity as an adult athlete, not as the kid you used to be.

> Have you had children? Sorry, but that changes your body forever. Don't use numbers that predate childbirth.

> Have you been building muscle in the gym? Chances are you want to hang on to it.

> Likewise, if you have put on significant weight since your youth, you have also gained muscle (to move your bigger body around). It may not be possible to get back to that old weight without getting rid of a significant amount of muscle.

> Are you nearing 50 or beyond? Higher body fat is an unavoidable consequence of age. The number that worked for you in your 20s and 30s is not going to work in your 50s, 60s, or 70s.

If a number from your past is no longer suitable, find a new one—a better one.

Consider the Skin You're In

When you lose weight, your body shrinks, and it can take some time for your skin to catch up. If you are over 40, it may never shrink back, and you will be left with some saggy skin. You might have to choose between being lean and wrinkly or chubby and smooth. In some cases, cosmetic surgery is the only way to get rid of the excess.

If you are all about performance, let your skin do what it wants and get as lean as you can.

Set Your Body Composition Goal

Get your body fat tested (and look up your BMI) when you begin your program. The heavier you are, the less accurate the body-fat tests will be, but it is still worth doing. If for no other reason, it will force you to find a facility for testing as you progress. Avoid the temptation to diet down to the lowest possible starting level. Dehydration doesn't help you much as it will actually decrease the readings for lean body mass.

ESTIMATE A TIMELINE

It is nice to know approximately how long it will take for you to reach your goal weight. You can assume ½ pounds of weight loss per week, or you can be more precise and use the online calculator discussed below.

Dynamic Calorie Model

In 1958, researcher Max Wishnofsky, MD, calculated that 1 pound of fat stores approximately 3,500 kcal of energy. Until only recently, we thought that creating a 3,500-calorie deficit would result in a 1-pound weight loss. All we had to do was figure out how many pounds we wanted to lose, and then we could do the math to arrive at a rate of weight loss for a given amount of calorie restriction. This model has proven to be a dismal failure because it assumes a consistent amount of weight loss week to week. Reality has shown that is not the case.

It is now widely known that the body's energy requirements decrease and physiological adaptations occur when you diet, so the rate of weight loss declines and sometimes comes to a screeching halt, even when you are following it precisely.

There are weeks when you will lose a surprising amount of weight and weeks when the scale (undeservedly) goes up. Plateaus, dips, and climbs are the order of the day. It is typical to lose faster in the first week or two before things level off. On average you should take in enough calories that you will lose ½ to 2 pounds a week, a safe and effective rate of weight loss. If you lose significantly more than this, you increase the magnitude of your body's adaptation to the calorie restriction. In other words, your body will be shocked and will object strenuously by slowing metabolism more than if your calorie restriction was modest. Even in a best case scenario, your weight loss will not be linear; it will fluctuate up and down.

Fig. 9 Nonlinear weight loss

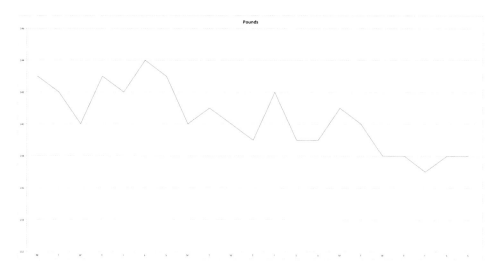

The 3,500 calorie rule sets us up for failure when it doesn't work or when it stops working once the dieter reaches a dreaded plateau. But don't worry. The era of a new mathematical model is upon us. Researchers at the mathematical biology section of the National Institutes of Health have developed a calculator that allows for more detailed input about training load and take into account age, sex, and other factors in predicting the rate of weight loss. (See Hall et al., 2016.)

This new calculator takes into account the slowing metabolism and other changes that occur as you reduce calorie intake so that you can predict rate of weight loss more accurately. The researchers that developed the model found that

➤   the **bodyweight** response to a reduction in calories is slower than one would expect (it takes about twice as long to lose each pound than the old 3,500 calorie model predicts); and

> people who are more overweight lose more weight for a given calorie reduction than those who are less overweight, which is consistent with the difficulty in losing those "last 10 pounds".

Following are some pictures of the initial screen of the body-weight planner calculator (figure 10) as well as a website where you can learn more about it. You can set your activity levels and a reasonable calorie deficit, and it will tell you how long the weight loss will take.

Setting Activity Levels and Baseline Calories

You can use the planner to determine your baseline calories and to estimate how long it will take to reach your goal weight.

1. First, determine your baseline calorie levels without including your training. Once you have this baseline number, write it down and remember it. It will be your guide for the rest of your life.

You will need additional calories if you are training, but you will add those according to specific guidelines discussed later.

2. Next, you will add your average weekly training load into the activity levels.

Now work through the calculator assuming a 300-500 calorie per day deficit. This should give you an approximate date for reaching your goal.

This planner also allows you to plan your maintenance level calories. Once you get there, this will help to keep you within 2 pounds of your goal weight for the six-week maintenance phase.

Fig. 10 Entry screen of body-weight planner

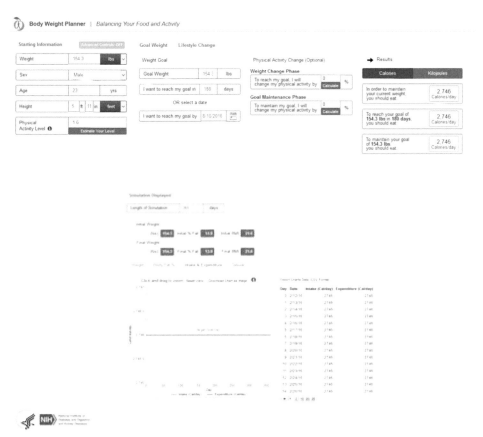

Visit to use the planner.

This model is helpful but not required for planning your timeline. You will stay in the weight-loss phase as long as it takes to reach your goal weight.

Victory Races

Being self-conscious about how you look in triathlon clothes might be one of the things that motivates you to get lean. Let's face it, fear of embarrassment is among the strongest motivators. You can use that your advantage by registering now for a series of short races, starting just a month from now. The races must be short so you have a relatively light training load to keep you focused on food (not training hours) for weight loss. The race must also be soon enough that you need to start losing weight immediately so that you will look leaner on race day.

You can do a race every four to six weeks to keep you motivated. It does not have to be a triathlon. Running is tremendously impacted by weight, so expect to be running faster with every pound you lose. Climbing on the bike should also improve dramatically (assuming you are training hard, too). Although you will certainly look leaner in your swimsuit, your swimming probably will not improve as you lose weight.

Look forward to celebrating your success with each race. Look forward to the race photos. If you order a photo from each race, you will be able to see your progress. By all means, do a race near the date you expect to reach your final goal, too. By then, you will need a new race kit in a smaller size.

CHAPTER 5:
WORKING YOUR PLAN

"A good plan is like a road map: it shows the final destination and usually the best way to get there."

–H. Stanely Judd

BE PREPARED FOR THE LONG HAUL

Losing the weight is certainly the goal, but to achieve lifetime weight control, you need to take a broader view and recognize that getting to your goal weight is just the beginning.

According to the National Weight Control Registry (NWCR), maintaining a 10% weight loss beyond one year is rare. Unfortunately, only about 20% of the population will achieve it. How many of your races have an 80% dropout rate?

The metabolic slowdown that occurs during weight loss will stick with you for up to one year, so you must remain exceptionally vigilant about your eating for a long time beyond the happy day when you reach your goal.

On the positive side, once weight loss is maintained for two to five years, the chances of longer-term success are much better. When you achieve that, you will become part of a small but exceptional population that is being tracked by the NWCR. If you sign up on their website, you will be able to participate in ongoing studies of successful weight losers.

There are three steps to lifetime weight control:

1. Losing the weight
2. Maintaining the weight for six weeks
3. Stabilizing at your new weight

Each Stage has ups and downs, and at times, you will go back to an earlier stage in order to lose a few pounds (figure 11). There is really no endpoint to this process. As humans, our lives change constantly, and maintaining your weight will be easy at times and harder at other times. The saving grace is that as time goes by it becomes easier.

Fig. 11 Stages of lifetime weight management

Weight-loss phase (until you reach weight goal)	Maintenance phase (6 weeks or more)	Stabilizing phase (1 year)
Tightly controlled calorie intake and lots of structure. The more rules you apply, the more successful you will be.	Find maintenance level calories by increasing calorie intake slightly and monitoring weight closely. Reduce calories back to the weight-loss phase level if your weight goes up more than 2 pounds.	Remove some structure as rules have become second nature. Continue maintenance level calorie intake. Return to maintenance level if your weight goes up more than 3 pounds.

PHASE ONE: WEIGHT LOSS

This is the part most people focus on. It is the most exciting because you will see striking change, and others will notice it, too. You will be making dramatic changes in your diet and in your environment, so along with the excitement, there will be plenty of stress. There are many rules to follow, and these rules build lots of structure into your eating life. People will notice that you are doing something different, so social pressure will be at its highest. You will jump on the scale with gleeful anticipation in the early weeks when you will see the biggest changes in your weight. This part of the process also requires the most energy and the most endurance, but as a triathlete, you have plenty of both.

During the weight-loss phase, you will

➤   determine your baseline calorie level (chapter 4);

➤   change your diet (chapter 6);

➤   practice your brain training (chapter 7) every day;

➤   use the rules and tools in chapter 8;

➤   fuel your training as described in chapter 9;

➤   incorporate strength training into your workouts; and

➤   add some high-intensity training to every workout.

Stick With Your Goal

Focus on reaching your target weight, no matter what. Do not allow yourself to be distracted from this goal. Follow your food plan, train your body and brain, and follow the rules until you reach your destination.

It may be tempting to modify your goal along the way, especially when you hit a plateau and weight loss slows or comes to a screeching halt. You might decide to settle for the weight loss you have already achieved, or worse, to take a break and save the big push for those last pounds for a later time. Either one of these decisions will ultimately lead to a catastrophic deflation of your motivation. If you settle for less than the big dream, you will sell yourself short, you won't reap the benefits of being at your goal weight, and you will have accepted failure once again. Every time you break a promise to yourself, you chip away at your self-respect. Your goal was well considered, and you chose it for a reason.

I can't emphasize enough the importance of pushing through and achieving your dream weight. You have no idea how motivating it is to get rid of all the extra weight—you will have muscle definition that you have never seen before. You will start to look really athletic rather than just "not overweight."

When you are working very hard to achieve a formidable goal, your psyche directs exceptional resources to the endeavor. These resources include dreams, motivation, fantasy, patience, and a little fear as well. Your goal has to be a gigantic goal—like reaching the Ironman finish line. You must invest so much into it that you will not tolerate failure. That is why choosing a motivating and exciting goal is so important.

If you were doing an Ironman race, and five miles from the finish you decided it was no longer a worthy goal and you quit, how would you feel the next day? How would you feel about that choice for years to come? Pain is temporary; pride is forever. And this applies to reaching your goal weight, too. Reaching your goal is every bit as important for your sense of self-worth and power as an Ironman finish line is. Your goal weight is your Ironman finish Line. You must not fail!

In lifetime weight management, achieving a goal weight is a victory that will set other victories in motion. Reaching it will change how you see yourself. It will change your life. You must do it!

Plateaus

One of the changes that occurs during weight loss is that your body burns fewer calories, even as you exercise. The more frequently you have dieted, the harder it can be to lose weight. This frustrating aspect of weight control is being actively studied, and the science says that it has to do with more than just carrying around less weight. The body adapts to calorie deficits in several ways, all of which serve to maintain a baseline body weight and to return to that weight if you go below it. This is why those last few pounds (the ones that will transform your athletic look the most) can be so hard to lose.

➤ Loss in muscle causes a slowing basal metabolic rate known as adaptive thermogenesis.

➤ Energy expenditure from the process of ingesting, absorbing, metabolizing, and storing nutrients from food is reduced because you are eating less of it.

➤ There is less "non-exercise" movement, such as fidgeting or moving around at your desk, walking more slowly, and bending down less often.

➤ There are hormonal responses like reduced thyroid levels which reduce metabolic rate. Studies show a host of hormonal changes that accompany weight loss.

➤ Adaptations in mitochondrial efficiency reduce the amount of energy used by working muscles.

The body-weight planner discussed in chapter 4 takes these plateaus into account, helping you manage your expectations. If you hit a plateau, don't despair. Stay the course and be patient. It could take a while to emerge from the standstill. As long as you are working your plan and eating as little as possible to do what you need to do in life, then that is all you can do. Quitting is not an option. Accepting your plateau weight as your new goal weight is not an option.

Incorporate Strength Training

Strength training will reduce the amount of muscle loss which can be as high as 25% of your initial weight loss. This muscle loss contributes to plateaus in weight loss. So spending extra time in the gym, or better yet, incorporating muscle-building exercises into your swims, runs, and rides (see figure 12), will pay big dividends.

The many benefits of functional strength training are described in detail in Strength Training for Triathletes (Meyer and Meyer, 2012). Be sure to read it.

Fig. 12 How to incorporate functional strength exercises into a run

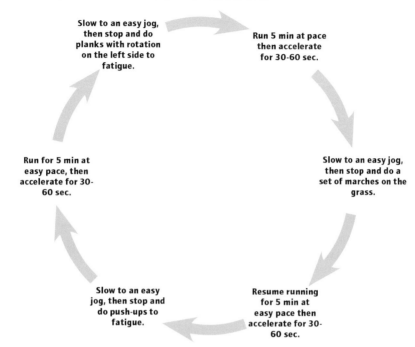

Slow to an easy jog, then stop and do planks with rotation on the left side to fatigue.

Run 5 min at pace then accelerate for 30-60 sec.

Slow to an easy jog, then stop and do a set of marches on the grass.

Run for 5 min at easy pace, then accelerate for 30-60 sec.

Resume running for 5 min at easy pace then accelerate for 30-60 sec.

Slow to an easy jog, then stop and do push-ups to fatigue.

Here is an example of how to incorporate functional strength work into a 30- to 45-minute run. You need an area that has some flat grass and maybe a railing or sturdy bench that you can lean on. Run at an easy pace to warm up for about 10 minutes, and then stop and do the first exercise to failure. That means do it until you can't execute it correctly anymore. Then stand up and run a few minutes to get your breath back. Then begin to accelerate and hold a fast run pace for about 30 to 60 seconds. Slow to a jog to recover, and then do the next exercise—again to failure. Continue like this until you have done one set of each exercise. Now finish your run at an easy to moderate pace. If you track this workout on your GPS device, you will see the spikes in heart rate during the fast running and the exercises.

➢ Do push-ups on the ground or against a railing, balance on one leg to make it harder. Keep your elbows against your sides. Make the push-ups easier by keeping your knees on the ground.

➤ Perform bridges and marches (figure 13). Keep your hips level while lifting each leg, keeping the knee bent. Place your hands on the ground to stabilize you and make the exercise easier; place your hands over your head to make it harder.

Fig. 13 Bridges (left) and marches (right) can be done with feet on a stability ball or on the ground.

➤ Plank Variations: Three basic plank variations are a plank with four contact points— toes and elbows (figure 14); plank with three contact points, lifting either one foot or one arm off the ground (figure 15); and plank with two contact points, lifting one leg and opposite elbow off the ground. Another variation is a side plank with rotation (figure 16). With two contact points—elbow and same-side foot—reach left arm to the sky then forward and underneath you while holding yourself up on your side.

Fig. 14 Basic plank (shown with suspension device) can be done outdoors with toes and elbows on the ground, providing four contact points.

Fig. 15 Plank with three contact points (two feet and one elbow)

Fig. 16 Side plank with rotation (pictured using suspension trainer) can be be done with feet and elbow on the ground, providing two contact points.

> Pilates hundred: Lie on your back with legs bent at 90 degrees. Your thighs should be perpendicular to the ground and away from the chest. Lower legs should be parallel to the ground, forming a table top (i.e., hips and knees at 90 degrees). Engage your deep abdominals and round your lower spine into the ground. Exhale and lift your upper back off the ground until the bottom tips of your shoulder blades are just off the floor. Reach your arms toward your feet and pump your hands up and down using a tiny range of motion and keeping the elbows straight. Inhale for five arm pumps and exhale for five pumps until you reach 100 repetitions.

➤ Curb jumps: Find a low curb or step and jump onto it and back down with both feet. If you pause for just long enough to lose momentum, you will be building strength, which is helpful in the base and building phases of your race training. As you near race day, doing this exercise with more of a spring action and no pause will build power, improving your sprint as you run down the finishing chute.

Strength Training During Rides and Swims

Hill climbing is strength work for cycling and running. The faster you go up a hill, the greater the training load, so don't expect to get noticeably stronger by just spinning up hills in an easy gear.

Big gear work challenges the legs even further, but be careful as this puts a big strain on the joints.

You can also mix things up by using a resistance band on the trainer or stationary bike, as shown in figures 17 and 18. You need two anchor points, one low and one higher. Use a light band as these are very challenging exercises.

Fig. 17 Prone pull-backs on stationary bike

Fig. 18 Rotation pull-back and prone Y on the stationary bike

Sprinkle these moves into a trainer session or do them all at the end. One set of each to failure will do the trick.

To add a strength component to the swim, swim against a tether anchored on a lane attachment, handrail, or starting block (figure 19). Tethers provide high resistance, pulling you backward when you extend the cord. If your swim technique is poor, tether swimming can injure your shoulders, so use it with caution. Be sure to get one that anchors at the waterline. Some models anchor above the water and pull you up, which is awkward.

Start out with just a few intervals of 30 strokes with a full recovery period and build from there. Think of the tether as a heavy weight and use it accordingly. You should avoid swimming for prolonged periods (20 minutes or more) against the tether.

Fig. 19 Swim tether

Another resistance device for swimmers is the parachute (figure 20). You can purchase these in various sizes. The smallest size is a good place to start. The parachute creates an enormous amount of resistance that helps you build strength. It slows your stroke down so you can improve your technique as well. Parachutes can be used in open water and pools swims and are easier on the shoulders. Think of them as lighter weights than the tether, so you can use them for up to 30 minutes continuously.

As with any device, be cautious. If you feel discomfort, back off.

Fig. 20 Swim parachute

Incorporate High-Intensity Training

"Go anaerobic every day" is the motto of Ironman legend Lew Hollander (figure 21). Lew is in his 80s and still competing in Ironman events. He is also on to something. Research has shown that high-intensity interval training (HIIT) improves both aerobic and anaerobic fitness and improves body composition better than low-intensity training. The workouts that have been tested are very short—about 20 minutes, 3 to 4 times per week—and they can, and may already, be part of your regular training program. It makes sense to start incorporating HIIT into your training schedule so you can get leaner and faster at the same time. Even run-of-the-mill interval training (high speed, high effort for durations up to 20 minutes) should be part of your training in every phase (base, build, and peak), although in differing amounts.

Note that the initial HIIT studies have been on sedentary, non-athletes. So the results are likely to be the most dramatic in triathletes who are either new to the sport or have spent very little time training at high intensity. Seasoned triathletes who have included high-intensity workouts in their training for years have already developed the cellular changes brought about by this kind of training, so they will not see as much benefit.

Since running at high intensity is hard on the muscles and more likely to lead to injury, start with doing your HIIT on the bike. You can do it on your indoor trainer, on a spin bike, or out on the road.

If you want to incorporate some high intensity into your running, start with combining a run with a few functional strength.

Fig. 21. Lew Hollander (Photo used with permission by Lew Hollander)

Here are some examples of HIIT that you can incorporate into your training following a 10-minute warm-up:

> Pedal as hard as you can in a moderate gear for 30 seconds; then recover for 30 seconds. Repeat 4 to 6 times.

> Pedal as hard as you can for 8 seconds; recover for 20 seconds. Repeat for 20 minutes.

> Pedal as hard as you can for 15 seconds; recover for 15 sec. Repeat for 20 minutes.

PHASE TWO: MAINTENANCE

Once you have reached your goal weight, move directly to maintenance (figure 22). This is the phase you have probably skipped in the past. Maintenance as the most critical part of the process. It is now that you will test the waters and start to live a less structured food life, without regaining any of the weight back. In the next 6 weeks you will:

➤ Reevaluate your baseline calorie level.

➤ Continue to practice your brain training (chapter 7) every day.

➤ Move to weekly, rather than daily, weigh-ins.

➤ Fuel your training as described in chapter 9.

➤ Stay focused on holding your weight steady.

Maintenance Means Less Structure and Adding Calories

By all means, celebrate your accomplishment and bask in your success. Buy some new clothes. Do something to commemorate the day. You have entered the chute to the finish line and you are going to make it!

Fig. 22 Maintenance phase

Maintenance Phase (6 weeks or more)						
Maintenance weight (+2 lb):						
BMI/Body composition:						
Baseline calories:						
Maintenance calories:						
Victory race dates:						

This is a critical time. It may be tempting to back away from your program for a few days to take a break, but don't! Continue to do all of the things you did in stage one to reach your goal. Keep following your plan; stick with the rules that have been helpful along the way. As you will shift from losing weight to maintaining it, you can eat a little more. Add up to 200 calories to your baseline calories. If your weight stays the same, you have reached your new normal calorie intake. If you continue to lose weight, go ahead and add another 200 calories a day, and so on, until your weight stabilizes. Watch your weight very carefully. If you creep above your goal weight, you will have to redouble your efforts to get back down and hold it for six more weeks.

Go ahead and increase your training load if you wish. For all intents and purposes, you have arrived at your new lifelong baseline calorie target. It may take you several tries to be able to hold your weight for six weeks.

This stage will allow your body to adapt to its new size and weight, and you can expect to regain some of the muscle you lost. At the end of this stage, have your body fat tested and, by all means, enter another race and test out the new machine. See how it feels.

PHASE THREE: STABILIZING

This final phase will last up to one year (figure 23). It begins after you have achieved phase 2, maintaining your weight loss without gaining more than two pounds for six consecutive weeks. At this point, you have probably come further in your weight control journey than ever before. You have a strong grasp of what it takes to lose weight and, for the most part, how to keep it off. But what you still lack is confidence that you can hold on to your new weight no matter what, and you might also feel that your new weight is not really "you" yet.

During the stabilizing phase you will:

➤ Eat at your maintenance calorie level.

➤ Reinforce your brain training constantly.

➤ Use the rules and tools that matter most.

➤ Keep training and racing and loving your sport!

➤ Stay attentive to your weight.

Fig. 23 Stabilizing phase

Stabilizing Phase (one year)
Lifetime weight range (5 lb):
Body composition range:
Baseline calories
Maintenance calories:
Victory races:

Get rid of the clothes that no longer fit you. Plan a future with certainty that you will remain lean. Live with your new self for a while. Your metabolism will take up to a year to adjust to this new weight. It will slowly speed up so you will eventually be able to eat a little more-but not too much. You need to add another belief to your list, and that is the belief that this is your new "Normal Weight". It is not a temporary state. It is forever, for as long as you want it to be by continuing to apply all that you have learned about weight control.

If you get injured or for some reason you can't train, you know you will be alright because it wasn't the training that took the weight off, it was your attention to food. You will be able to maintain your weight with much less focus on all those rules, but some of them will have to stay in place. By now you know what they are.

No Shortcuts

Wouldn't it be nice if you could have taken a shortcut? If you could have taken a magic pill and be at your goal weight tomorrow, imagine the effort you would save! But just think of all the changes you have made in the way you think about yourself and about food. A shortcut would have skipped all that. If your body changed without the brain training that goes along with it, you would be right back to your starting weight in no time. This is what happens to people that focus only on what they eat. By working on your thoughts and beliefs, you are in a much stronger place now, and it will be easier to stay lean.

If You Gain Weight

As soon as your weight begins to climb, go back to maintenance level calories and follow those rules. If you nip it in the bud, it will not take long to get back down to your normal weight. Don't be upset by a small weight gain. You will gain weight and lose it again many times for the rest of your life. As long as act immediately when you put on a few pounds, you will be alright. Take these normal weight fluctuations in stride. The various rules set out for phase one are always there for you when you need them. Your body is always changing, so don't expect to stay rock solid on a single number for the rest of your life. Just stay vigilant and go back to what works when you need to.

Retest Body Composition

What is your body composition at your goal weight? Schedule follow-up body composition tests every six months, and rely on your scale to keep your weight stable between evaluations.

Give yourself some leeway. If it was difficult to stay at your goal number for six weeks, consider using that number as your new goal. Give yourself a five-pound range of acceptable weight. Monitor it carefully, and if your weight goes above the range, immediately go back to the calorie target that worked for you. The sooner you jump on the weight gain, the easier it will come off. This is the prime benefit of weighing yourself every week.

In the months and years to come, your weight may fluctuate a few pounds even though you maintain the same body-fat levels. If you seem to be putting on weight and returning to your baseline calorie target does not take it away, don't despair, it is time for another body composition test.

The Miracle of Your Stable Weight

By now, you have developed so many weight management skills for so long that they are natural. When you are eating well without starving; you are able to train and race; and your weight is staying put, you will have reached the happy place known as a healthy, stable weight. Have you ever achieved that before? It is an astonishing place.

This is the point when you can look happily in the mirror and realize...you did it!

PART FOUR:
WHAT TO EAT, BRAIN TRAINING, RULES AND TOOLS

CHAPTER 6:
WHAT TO EAT

"Eating crappy food isn't a reward—it's a punishment."

–Drew Carey

FOODS TO AVOID

Now we will finally get to the nitty-gritty. Figure 25 shows the foods that you should avoid because they carry significant health risks, are high in calories and very low in nutritional value. They area also high calorie density foods so for weight loss reasons alone, they should be avoided.

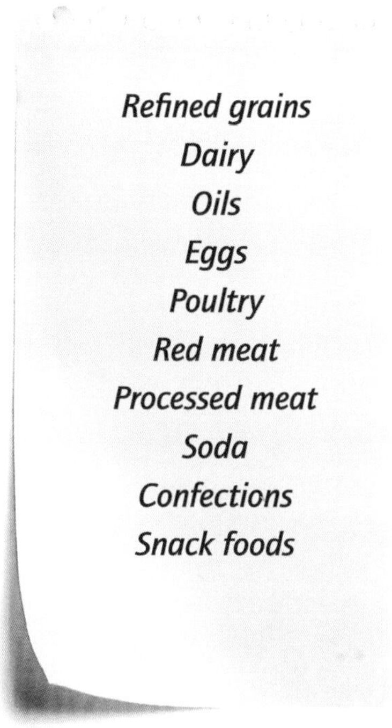

Refined grains
Dairy
Oils
Eggs
Poultry
Red meat
Processed meat
Soda
Confections
Snack foods

Fig. 25 Foods to avoid

A plant-based diet is a good option as it allows you to consume nutritious foods as well as to feel full and satisfied. It also will help you achieve your weight-loss goal. Figure 26 shows one triathlete's plant-based diet.

Rather than attempt to change your entire diet overnight, it is much more effective to alter your current diet in a way that appeals most to you. If, for example, you absolutely must have a bag of potato chips every week, you can work with that. You might decide those chips aren't really worth the price in terms of calories and cravings for more, but that is your decision to make. Once you have worked through this chapter, you will have a clear picture of what you should be eating and what you should avoid.

Fig. 26 A triathlete's plant-based diet

This is what a simple weekday might look like for a triathlete eating a plant-based diet.

Breakfast: Black coffee

Hot oatmeal with unsweetened almond milk, bananas, dates, blueberries, pepitas, and walnuts

Post-workout snack: Handful of raw almonds

Lunch: Whole-grain pasta with tomato sauce, topped with extra vegetables

Tangerine

Afternoon/Pre-workout snack:

Banana

Kale and fruit smoothie

Fuel during evening workout:

Red licorice pieces

Lemonade

Recovery meal: Almonds and raisins

Dinner: Brown rice and refried beans on whole wheat Tortilla with taco sauce

Grapes

Evening Snack: Natural peanut butter and strawberry spread on whole-grain English muffin

CALORIE DENSITY

People tend to eat a consistent amount of food from day to day. The amount is based on food weight, not calories. An effective calorie-reducing plan will cut calories without reducing the amount (weight) of food you can eat. This is done by eating less high-calorie density (HCD) food and more low-calorie density (LCD) food. Calorie density describes the number of calories per mouthful.

The foods that put on weight are the same ones that tend to have very little nutritional value and they are HCD foods. But you don't have to give up all HCD foods, you just need to be careful with them.

Weight management becomes relatively easy once you learn how to combine HCD and LCD foods so that you can eat what you enjoy and eat enough to satisfy your appetite. You can apply these skills to any food, but HCD foods are the most important ones to manage. Here are the things you can do with HCD foods:

Limit: Just eat less of it.

Substitute: Find a lower calorie alternative.

Modify: Mix in some low-calorie food to dilute calorie density and to learn to enjoy new, healthier food tastes.

Before you can use these three skills, you have to know which foods are HCD and which ones aren't. The best way to start is to learn about the foods you typically eat. Keeping your diet familiar is less stressful than adopting an entirely new one. Although making a food list takes some extra effort it is worth doing a truly custom food program.

MAKE A FOOD LIST

The food list will help you identify which foods are high in calorie density and which ones are low. Once you have done this, you can decide which foods to be careful with when eating.

There are many online calculators and food lists to ease the process of looking up calorie and fat counts for the foods you have listed. These include: www.nutritiondata.com, www.thedailyplate.com, www.freedieting.com, and www.caloriecontrol.org. Creating an online food log is helpful, but you should either print it out or make a hard copy like figure 27 to keep in your kitchen, car, and office. You will need access to the information whenever a food issue arises.

Once you have completed the worksheet, you can identify the HCD foods (calorie bombs) and the LCD foods (calorie bargains).

How to complete the food list (figure 27):

List all of the foods in each category that you typically eat, and then record the calories and fat grams per serving.

Combination foods like casseroles are difficult. The best way is to look up each ingredient separately, but don't count the vegetables or spices. The only vegetable worth counting is potatoes. Count all the other ingredients.

Assume that fat-based sauces, dressings, and toppings (that contain cream, cream soups, butter, and oil) have 120 calories per tablespoon.

Fig. 27 Food list

Food type	Calories per serving
Breads, bakery items, pastries	
Pasta, rice, grains, warm and cold cereals	
Fruits, juices—dried and frozen	
Butter, oil, shortening, sauces, toppings, dips	
Fast food	
Takeout food	
Beef	
Chicken	
Fish	
Processed meats—sausage, cold cuts, deli	
Dairy—cheeses, yogurt, milk, eggs	
Vegetables—canned, fresh, frozen	
Soups	
Casseroles, stews, combination foods	
Desserts, pastries, candy, chocolates, pie, cake, ice cream	
Nut milks (e.g., soy and almond)	
Nuts, nut spreads	
Drinks, sodas, juices	

Food type	Calories per serving
Snack foods	
Beans, lentils, soy products	
Other	
Training fuels—carbohydrate/electrolyte replacements, gels, bars, recovery shakes	

Once you have completed your list, you should identify which foods are high-calorie density. HCD foods are those that

1. exceed 10 grams of fat per serving or
2. exceed 300 calories per serving.

The HCD foods are the ones you will limit, substitute, or modify as explained next. That does not mean you have to stop eating them, only that you must manage them to reduce their calorie impact. The skills described in the next section will help you do that.

EATING BETTER

Learning to limit, substitute, or modify will help you manage the HCD foods on your food list and any others you encounter.

The skills can be applied however you wish. There is no single correct way to manage any particular food. You can limit, substitute, or modify any food. When you want to eat a HCD food, ask yourself:

1. Do I want really want to eat it? (limit)
2. If yes, is it a food I can substitute with a LCD alternative? (substitute)
3. If not, can I combine it with other LCD foods to reduce the calorie density? (modify)

Some HCD foods will be easy for you to avoid or limit, whereas others are so central to your diet that you feel deprived without them. Some foods are easy to modify by combining them with LCD foods to dilute their calorie density. Still, other foods are convenient and satisfactory to substitute. You decide which action to take.

Now that you have identified the HCD foods in your diet, figure 28 has suggestions for applying the three skills to those foods.

Fig. 28 What to do with HCD foods

Common HCD foods	Plant-based ways to limit, substitute, or modify
Alcohol	Avoid or limit to once a week. Add fresh fruit to make a sangria. White wine and light beer are less calorie dense.
Baked sweets (commercially made)	Substitute with homemade and modify using 50% less oil or shortening. Better yet, substitute applesauce for most of the oil and use date sugar instead of any other sweetener.
Butter, mayonnaise, salad dressings	Use very small amounts. Substitute or modify with mustard, salsa, fruit juice, or balsamic or other flavored vinegars. Tofu and tahini make great sauce bases.

Common HCD foods	Plant-based ways to limit, substitute, or modify
Canned frosting	Avoid as much as possible. These products are nearly 100% fat. Substitute with homemade or with flavored syrups and light whipped topping.
Cheese-based Italian foods—pizza, lasagna, cheese or garlic bread, cheese sauce	Remove most cheese or serve on whole-grain bread and pasta products; add fresh tomato, green pepper, garlic, zucchini, mushrooms, and onion.
Cheese-heavy Mexican food	Add more lettuce, tomato, and salsa. Remove cheese. Prepare beans without lard. Use brown rice instead of white.
Carbohydrate and protein bars, powders, and drinks	OK if consumed during workouts. Otherwise, substitute with real food*.
Doughnuts and pastries	Avoid or limit. Modify by mixing small pieces with fruit.
Dried fruit	Fresh fruits provide more bulk and satiety, but dried fruit is extra sweet and makes a nice mix-in or topping.
Fast food	Choose plant-based side dishes that are not fried. Avoid cheese and mayonnaise-based sauces.
Fried foods—meats, potatoes, vegetables	Choose roasted, baked, broiled, boiled, or steamed. Better yet, sautée in water, wine, or vegetable broth.
Dairy products—cream, milk, cottage cheese, yogurt, ice cream	Substitute with nut milk-based products.
Nuts, nut butters	Use natural versions without added sugar and salt. Use sparingly. In the context of a plant-based diet, nuts are a staple and a hearty substitute for animal proteins and junk food. Although calorie dense, whole nuts are poorly absorbed during digestion, so many of the calories pass through the system unused.

Common HCD foods	Plant-based ways to limit, substitute, or modify
Processed meat, including hot dogs, sausage, deli meat, beef jerky, bacon, and more. Processed meat is meat that has been transformed through salting, curing, fermentation, smoking, or other processes to enhance flavor or improve preservation.	Avoid processed meat if you can. The World Health Organization has deemed these foods carcinogenic (cancer causing).
Soda, sweetened beverages, fruit juices	Substitute with water or nut milk-based, blended salad without added protein powder, which is usually mostly sugar.
Visible fat or skin on any cut of meat	Avoid. Remove skin (after cooking), and drain fat before making sauces.

*See *Power Hungry: The Ultimate Energy Bar Cookbook* by Camilla V. Saulsbury (Lake Isle Press, 2013) and *Feed Zone Portables: A Cookbook of On-the-Go Food for Athletes* by Biju Thomas and Allen Lim (Velo Press, 2013).

Canned Food Is Fine

Don't feel that you must cook everything from scratch. Canned beans, fruits, and vegetables are perfectly fine, and they are very convenient. You are better off choosing the low sodium versions, but it is all right to start with the regular versions. Grocery stores are starting to carry portable versions of canned goods in durable bags, so you can eat smaller amounts on the run instead of having to struggle with a can opener. Canned food is already cooked, which, in many cases, increases their nutritional value.

Canned fruit (in water) is delicious in smoothies, and you should always have some on hand. Using canned fruit gives you access to all sorts of flavors even when the fruit is out of season.

Frozen fruit is perfect for making smoothies. Keep a large variety in your freezer. If you need some sweet juice, defrost some of the fruit in the microwave and use the softened fruit and juice.

HOW TO LIMIT YOUR FAVORITE HCD FOOD

Limiting a food does not mean you have to eliminate it. It means eat as little of it as possible. Here are some ways to do that:

1. Don't keep the food in the house. If you must, go out and have it in a restaurant. Don't keep the leftovers.
2. If it ends up in your house, eat a single serving, and then immediately discard the leftovers.
3. Eat it as infrequently as possible.
4. Include it only as your recovery meal following your longest training session.

If you absolutely must eat a particular HCD food, pick the one that will give you the greatest satisfaction. Sometimes, the only food that will satisfy you is one particular brand. In that case, go ahead and eat it. There are times when a craving will not be satisfied any other way, and you can end up eating a large quantity (and more calories) of a poor substitute and still be left unsatisfied. If you are not married to one particular brand, look for the one that is the least calorie dense. That means you can eat more of it for a given number of calories.

You will be surprised how much variation there is among brands. Compare the labels and look at the following:

1. Which has the lowest number of calories per serving?
2. Which has the least amount of fat?
3. Which has the largest serving size?

Be careful with serving sizes. A quick glance at a label can make you think a food isn't too bad. The serving size for a high-calorie food is often smaller than a normal serving. Manufacturers label foods this way to mislead you into believing you are getting a lower calorie food.

The 10-Gram Rule

There is still some controversy over optimum daily fat intake, especially for athletes. But there is no reason to eat foods that are brimming with added fat. Read labels and avoid anything that has more than 10 grams of fat per serving. That said, you can still eat these foods, but in very limited quantities and on rare occasions. Since it is a HCD food, you will only be able to afford a bite or two, but it may be worth it. It is your call.

High-Calorie Density Starches and Desserts

A normal size chocolate chip cookie usually does not exceed 10 grams of fat, but a pancake-sized one does. Low-fat and even some regular ice creams are within this limit. Slow-churned ice cream has less calorie density because it has extra air it, making it, literally, lighter by weight without adding artificial fats or sweeteners. Nonfat frozen yogurt is a good substitute, too.

If you decide you want ice cream or anything else that is calorie dense, read the labels until you find one that is acceptable from a fat standpoint. There are large brand-to-brand variations in the fat content of ice creams, frozen confections, candy bars (those with nuts and nut-based fillings are higher), baking mixes for cakes and cookies, pie crusts, and even breads. If you can't stay within the 10-gram rule, buy the lowest fat alternative available.

High-Calorie Density Fats

The 10-gram rule applies to more than desserts. What about fatty meat and cheese? Rather than eliminate these foods, eat them in small amounts to still get the most satisfaction from them. For example, a stew made with prime rib is a good way to add volume, but saturating the meat in a flavored sauce doesn't allow the taste of the beef to come through. If you are going to have prime rib or sausage or pizza, for that matter, eat a few bites that you will really enjoy.

Roasted chicken skin is tasty, but you can do without the fat. You can cook chicken without the skin, but it will be terribly dry. Instead, cook the chicken with the skin on to get some of the taste, and then remove it before eating or have a small piece of skin that you cut into tiny pieces. Have a little piece of skin with each bite of lean meat. Count the skin as a serving of fat.

Cheese is another example. Generally, flavor is enhanced in cold foods. Melted cheddar cheese does not taste as strong as cheese at room temperature. If you crave cheddar cheese, have it cold and separate it from other foods. Cheese sprinkled over a salad gets lost in the other flavors, so why bother? You can take this a step further and get the most flavor-intense option available. A small amount of sharp cheddar will give you more taste than mild cheddar will.

Avoid Caloric Drinks

Avoid liquid calories unless you are in the middle of a run or a bike ride, or if you need a recovery meal, but you don't feel like eating real food. Researchers have concluded that total calorie intake is significantly higher on days when you drink soda, alcohol, milk, and juice as opposed to the days when only water is consumed.

It makes sense. Liquids are heavy, but since they don't stay in your stomach very long, they don't contribute to the food weight you are used to consuming each day. They don't keep you satisfied. Your goal is to get the maximum satisfaction out of every calorie. When possible, eat the solid form instead of the liquid—an orange instead of orange juice, cottage cheese instead of milk.

Plain coffee and tea are calorie free, but be careful with what is added to them. A nonfat latte is very low in calories, but adding syrup and cream makes it into a calorie nightmare. Many varieties of tea are highly sweetened, so be careful.

Traditional smoothies are made with fruit juice, milk, and a host of added sugars and other things. If you make your own at home or are careful about ingredients in commercial smoothies, they are a great way to add vegetables to your diet. These are called blended salads.

You can use nut milks as a base, add fresh and frozen fruits (especially dates) for sweetness, add nuts and seeds for texture, and use any fruit or vegetable you have on hand. Here are a few recipes you can try.

BLENDED SALAD RECIPES

Chocolate Cherry

Ingredients:

- ½ cup almond milk
- 1 tbsp powdered, unsweetened cocoa
- Date sugar, to taste
- Frozen and defrosted or fresh black cherries

Peanut Butter Banana

Ingredients:

- ½ cup unsweetened almond or soy milk
- 1 tbsp natural peanut butter
- Date sugar to taste—add last
- Bruised/spotted banana—sweetness will vary, so taste after adding the banana

Cinnamon Apple Smoothie

Ingredients:

- 1 small apple, sliced
- 1/2 cup rolled oats
- 1/2 tbsp cinnamon
- 1/2 tbsp nutmeg
- 1 tbsp almond butter
- 1/2 cup unsweetened coconut milk
- 3-4 ice cubes
- 1/2 cup cold water

Directions:

Add the oats and water to your blender. Pulse a couple times and then allow the mixture to sit for at least 2-3 minutes so the oats can soften.

Add all the remaining ingredients to the blender. Process until smooth, about 30 seconds. Pour into a glass and sprinkle with a little extra cinnamon and nutmeg. Enjoy!

Eat Your Greens Smoothie

Ingredients:

- 3 oz baby spinach or kale

- 2 oz romaine lettuce

- 1 banana

- 1 cup frozen or fresh blueberries

- 1/2 cup unsweetened soy, hemp, or almond milk

- 1/2 cup pomegranate juice

- 1 tbsp ground flaxseeds

- Blend all ingredients in a high-powered blender until smooth and creamy.

- Avoid Oil

Any kind of oil that is added to foods and used in cooking adds virtually no nutritional value to the food. It only adds calories. Saturated fats are found in animal foods like dairy, cheese, and meat. Any kind of fat that stays solid at room temperature also stays solid in your arteries. Added plant oils, such as olive and canola oils, are liquid at room temperature, but they are still empty calories that you don't need. Yes, olives are a healthy food (when not brined to death adding huge amounts of salt), but when made into oil, most of the healthy components are discarded.

Most recipes call for oil. You can reduce the amount of added oil by two-thirds in most recipes, and you will not taste the difference. You can sauté vegetables using small amounts of water, vegetable broth, or wine. Heat the skillet first, and then add a small amount of liquid. Stir often and add more as needed.

When baking, reduce the oil by two-thirds by substituting some of the remaining oil with unsweetened applesauce.

Avoid bottled, commercial salad dressings. Rather, use flavored vinegars, salsa, fruit juices, spices, nuts, crushed avocado, tahini, and dried fruits in their place. You can get creative or just use what you have around. If you want a formal recipe, here are three super simple ones to start with.

PIQUANT DRESSING

Ingredients:

➤ 1/4 cup seasoned rice vinegar

➤ 1/4 cup salsa

➤ 1 garlic clove, pressed

BALSAMIC VINAIGRETTE

Makes 1/4 cup.

Ingredients:

- 2 tbsp balsamic vinegar
- 2 tbsp seasoned rice vinegar
- 1 tbsp ketchup
- 1 tbsp stone-ground mustard
- 1 garlic clove, pressed

FAT-FREE VINAIGRETTE

Makes about 1/2 cup.

Ingredients:

- 1/2 cup seasoned rice vinegar
- 1-2 tbsp stone-ground or Dijon mustard
- 1 garlic clove, crushed or pressed

SUBSTITUTIONS

Looking back at your food list, there are probably some foods that have more calories than you expected. There are three ways to substitute HCD foods:

1. Use the diet or low-calorie version of the food.
2. Use a lower fat version of the food.
3. Use a higher fiber (whole grain) or plant-based version of the food.

The easy way is to buy a diet product, but sometimes the low-calorie product is so tasteless it is not worth eating. Fat-free cheese is an example. If all you are looking for is texture, maybe the fat-free cheese will work, but if taste matters, you are better off eating a few shreds of real cheese.

Using vegetables as a substitute for starchy food is one of the best ways to dramatically reduce calories, increase nutrient value, and to stay fuller longer. Following are some examples of food substitutions. Use your food list for ideas and experiment. You can also find substitutions online at www.fitnessandfreebies.com, www.nhlbi.nih.gov, and www.goodhousekeeping.com.

When you can, substitute with a product that has more fiber, even if the calorie content is the same. Fiber is important because it does not digest, so it makes food bulky without adding calories. It takes longer to digest and literally keeps your stomach full longer. Fibrous fruits and vegetables and whole-grain products are examples of high-fiber foods. A growing selection of starchy carbohydrates (bread, pasta, cereal) are available in whole-grain versions.

THE 5:1 RULE

One way to tell if a product is truly whole grain and without too much added sugar is to read the label and divide the number of total carbohydrates by the number of grams of fiber. If the number is 5, that is a healthy product. If the number is 6 or 7, it is better than most. Figure 29 shows where to look on the label. This product has a 5:1 ratio of carbohydrate to fiber, so it is a good choice.

Fig. 29 Food label showing 5:1 ratio

Nutrition Facts	Amount/Serving	% Daily Value*	Amount/Serving	% Daily Value*
Serving Size 1 Slice (34g) Servings Per Container About 20	**Total Fat** 0.5g	1%	**Total Carb.** 15g	5%
	Saturated Fat 0g	1%	Dietary fiber 3g	11%
	Trans Fat 0g		Sugars 0g	
Calories 80	**Cholesterol** 0mg	0%	**Protein** 4g	8%
Calories from Fat 5	**Sodium** 75mg	3%	**Potassium** 80mg	
Calories from Saturated Fat 0				

Vitamin A 0% • Vitamin C 0%	• Calcium 0% • Iron 4%
Thiamine 8% • Magnesium 6%	• Niacin 6% • Vitamin B6 4%
Riboflavin 2% • Phosphurus 8%	• Zinc 4%

* Percent Daily Values are based on a 2,000 calorie diet.

MODIFICATIONS

Eating food that is different from what the rest of the family is eating is costly, stressful, and banishes you to a sort of social isolation. Eating normal food is an important skill that will allow you to fit in no matter where you are. But how do you minimize the calories? You modify the food so it is not so calorie dense. There are several ways to do this, and creativity can pay off. It will seem strange at first, but it gets easier and more interesting as time goes on. Here are some ways to modify normal food.

Remove HCD components:

➤ Remove skin and visible fats from meat.

➤ Remove cheese and fatty sauce.

Combine small portions of HCD food with larger volumes of LCD food:

➤ Here are some ways to add bulk to small portions of HCD main dish foods.

➤ Serve them in or on vegetables like shredded lettuce, shredded cabbage, bagged salad, spaghetti squash, stewed tomatoes, mushrooms, or celery.

➤ Make them into combination dishes like vegetable-based chili, casseroles, stews, and soups.

➤ Serve a tiny portion of HCD dessert with sugar-free angel food cake and fresh berries.

➤ Dilute the calorie impact of sauces, toppings, and dressings by using one-fourth the amount of high fat oil, butter, mayonnaise, or cream and mixing in some nonfat dairy, such as milk, yogurt, or sour cream. You have to experiment to find the proportions that preserve most of the taste.

CHAPTER 7:
BRAIN TRAINING

Suffer the pain of discipline, or suffer the pain of regret.

FACING YOUR TRUTH

Of successful weight losers, 83% report a triggering event that led to their weight loss The most common triggers are: a health threat, either a warning from their doctor or the death of a family member caused by an obesity-related problem; reaching an all-time high in weight; seeing an unflattering photo of themselves; and seeing their own reflection in the mirror.

Facing the truth about your weight situation can be painful. Have you faced your truth? It is personal to you. Someone else will not have the same feelings about your weight that you have. But we also have to live with ourselves and our beliefs and feelings.

Having the right weight and shape and being fit are important attributes in our culture. Like it or not, self-management, hard work, delay of gratification, and impulse control are qualities projected onto people with the "right" body.

Today's culture condemns "shaming" and we can see that it is a damaging and hurtful state of mind, but turning off your own inner voice isn't necessarily productive when deep in your soul you believe that your current weight is sapping the joy from your life. I tried to accept my weight and find beauty in it for years before deciding it was pointless to expend all this energy into talking myself out of something I wholeheartedly believed in.

I could be devoting the same energy to becoming what I wanted to be. I literally shamed myself into action and it has served me well.

Addicts call it "hitting bottom", when you reach a level of suffering so deep that it triggers a fundamental shift in thinking. The black box exercise may trigger those emotions in you, and that can be useful.

The Black Box Exercise

Your emotions about being overweight are wrapped in nebulous thoughts, memories, and beliefs. They have probably been haunting you for many years. If you are like most triathletes, you do your best to shut them away with more training and longer races. You have tried to diet them away, but diets are temporary, and when the weight comes back, the pain comes back, too.

Now is the time to come to terms what your weight problem has cost you. Now is the time to get angry and rise to the challenge. Now is the time to understand, on the deepest and most personal level, why you want to change.

‚When you do this exercise, you need to find some time to be alone. Turn off the phone, computer, and outside disturbances long enough to dive into the abyss and record what is there. You will need paper and a pen because you are going to write these things down on paper (not on a computer file).

You will never share these writings with anyone, so express yourself freely.

You are going to create a black box—a physical storehouse (symbolically black) for all of the unhappy truths about your weight. You are going to make a detailed list and put it into the box. The list can be on one sheet of paper or many small ones. Add photos if you like.

Write down all of the reasons you are dissatisfied with your current weight in precise detail. Tell the truth—the whole truth. What do you believe about yourself and your weight? Don't worry about if these things are objectively true.

Here are some examples:

> I hate it that I can't find clothes to fit. It makes me feel like I am the wrong shape and size, and I believe I am the wrong shape to be appealing to romantic partners.

> My relationship choices have been limited by my weight.

> I have missed many social events because I am self-conscious about my weight.

> I believe that others see me as weak, and I can't stand this.

> I believe that this weight makes me look much older than I am, and I hate that.

> I believe that looking like this shows that have given up on myself, and I have not.

> I believe that looking like this reflects that that I don't have the strength and willpower to say no to food, but I am so strong in other ways, and I don't accept this lack of strength and willpower in myself.

> I am embarrassed and ashamed of myself that I have not taken control of this aspect of my life.

> I feel like I am dragging around a ball and chain of weakness, and it makes me angry that this is of my own doing

- I can't forgive myself for allowing myself to be fat for another day.

- I am 40 years old, and I am only getting older. If I don't lose the weight now, I will never experience being a young and fit person. This is my last chance. If I lose the weight 10 years from now, I will have missed this chance.

- So many people have told me that I would be so beautiful if I just lost 20 pounds. I believe this is true.

- One of my friends even wrote about me as a character in their book, and they told me that my character in the book was overweight must like me. This was crushing.

- I have tried to accept myself this way—to embrace my shape. I have read books and meditated and performed all sorts of mental gymnastics. In the end, I simply do not accept myself this way. I do not WANT to accept myself this way. It is not what I want.

- Life is hard enough. We all have to deal with hardships outside our control. I can't accept this sadness when it is within my power to fix it.

- I deserve to be happy and to live my life without this issue—this sadness.

Once you get going, the momentum will reveal all sorts of memories. Write them down. Go with it! You might even cry. You might get really angry. Done right, this is an emotionally exhausting exercise.

When you have written it all down, take a deep breath and look again at your list. There will be a few statements that really cut you to the core. Those are the best ones. Those are the truths that matter most. Those are the ones that will drive you to change.

Take a little break. When you return, gaze upon the box. You will feel a pit in your stomach. The power of all of this negativity in one place is palpable. Do you feel it? If so, you have done your job well!

This box now contains all the emotions you have been hiding from all laid out in one place. If you start making changes right this moment, you don't ever have to revisit those truths. You can move forward. You can put the box on a shelf to remind you it is there, or you can hide it away. Do what suits you, but by all means, harness the power of those emotions to help you change how you deal with food. Feel the freedom of having let all those feelings out once and for all.

As long as you continue to move forward with your plan and with the practice of rewiring your brain, you can keep the box closed. You don't have to revisit those thoughts again. Ever.

THINK LIKE AN ATHLETE

Now that you know why you want to change your life, let's look at the mountain of positive attributes you already have as an athlete that will help you make those changes. These will guide you to your new lean destination. You already know that you can't out-train a bad diet, but you can use your athletic mindset to out-think it. It will be easier than you think because lifetime weight control is an athletic endeavor.

Let's get one thing straight right away: No matter how old you are, fast you are, or how new you are to the sport, if you are a person who is trained or skilled in exercises, sports, or games requiring physical strength, agility, or stamina, you are an athlete.

You already think like and athlete. Do you ever tell yourself these things?

1. I am physically and mentally strong.
2. I know how to push through when I am uncomfortable.
3. The more often I practice, the more skilled I become.
4. Athletes that have been training for many years are better at their sport than beginners.
5. I know that with training, I can improve my fitness, speed, and endurance.
6. I am persistent and determined. I never quit.
7. No matter what the circumstances, I will always find a way to be an athlete.
8. Being a triathlete is more than what I do—it is a lifestyle, it is who I am.
9. Training makes me feel powerful.
10. I am grateful that I can do this sport.

11. I am able to focus on a long-term goal or big race and work toward achieving it.
12. I get a lot of satisfaction out of knowing I am an athlete.
13. I know I have to train every day if I want to continue to improve.
14. If I stop training, I will lose the fitness I have achieved.
15. I love to train.
16. Every workout gets me a step closer to achieving my goals.
17. I surround myself with people that think the same way.
18. Remembering past victories makes me happy and energized.
19. I am excited about getting faster.

As an athlete with a weight problem, you probably suffer a disconnection between your athletic self and your weight-control self. You are proud of the discipline you show in training and embarrassed about your lack of discipline with food.

I challenge you to stop thinking of your weight management identity as something separate from your athletic self. Notice that the previous list does not include anything about how fast you are. Do you stop being an athlete because you achieve a personal best? Did you only enter one race in your life? Of course not. Being an athlete is a way of living. It is not a single race. As an athlete, you are invested in the process of achieving. You will seek new challenges for years to come, and you will keep getting better.

Expand those athletic thoughts (and attitude) into the realm of weight control. Focus on the process of being a (lifetime) weight controller, rather than on the end result of achieving a particular weight. Achieving a goal weight is only one step in the process of changing your weight identity.

Weight management is an athletic challenge, and the right mindset will make it the most satisfying one ever. It will transform you physically in a way that others can see; it will make you faster at your sport; and most important, it will do away with all that emotional baggage stewing away in your black box.

Here is the list of athletic beliefs expanded into the realm of weight management:

1. I am physically and mentally strong. My "not giving in" muscles are really strong, too.
2. I know how to push through when I am uncomfortable, even when I am hungry.
3. The more often I practice my sport and being powerful with food, the more skilled I become.
4. Athletes that have been training and staying lean for many years have more skill than newbies.
5. I know that by training my body, I can improve my fitness, speed, and endurance, and by training my brain, I can improve my body composition.
6. I am persistent and determined to manage my weight and to train hard. I never quit.
7. No matter what the circumstances, I will always find a way to be an athlete and to stay lean.
8. Being a lean triathlete careful about what I eat is more than what I do—it is a lifestyle, it is who I am.
9. Training and staying in control of my weight makes me feel powerful.
10. I am grateful that I can do this sport and that my physical challenges are things I can control.
11. I am able to focus on a long-term goal or big race and work toward achieving it.
12. I get a lot of satisfaction out of rewiring my brain and training my body.
13. I know I have to train every day if I want to continue to improve.
14. If I stop being vigilant about weight management and training, I will lose the fitness I have achieved.
15. I love being a lean triathlete.
16. Every workout, every powerful food thought and action gets me a step closer to achieving lifetime weight control.
17. I love to surround myself with other athletes that don't talk about "struggling," "trying," "fighting," or "suffering" with weight. Playing the victim is depressing and ineffective for any athletic endeavor.
18. Remembering past victories makes me happy and energized. The more food victories I accumulate, the stronger I become.
19. I am excited about getting stronger, faster, and leaner

When you read these statements, do they ring true? They apply as much when you are out on your bike as they do when you are in the grocery store or at a restaurant. Thinking like an athlete all the time lets you harness your discipline and resilience no matter where you are. So read these passages often, but especially right before you go out for dinner or to a social occasion that will include the temptation to overeat.

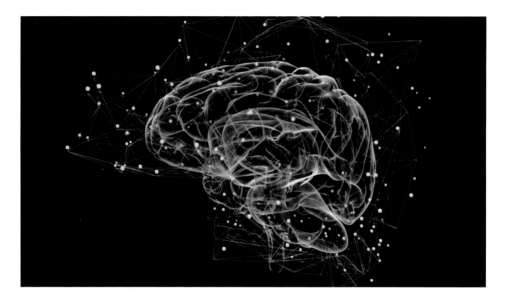

REWIRE YOUR BRAIN

Change Your Food Preferences

We all know what we should and should not eat, but we believe that eating healthy foods will not make us happy. Therefore, we will not be able to stick with a diet that deprives us of the foods we currently love.

This belief is incorrect. Eating healthy food will make you amazingly happy, and you will not feel deprived unless you choose to.

You can learn to be happy eating mostly the right foods, but it takes effort and time. You have to change the way you think if you expect to be able to eat in a different way than most everyone around you for the rest of your life. The tide is slowly turning, and perhaps in 10 years the world will be a different place, and the societal norms will support and reinforce healthy eating. Such a development would save countless lives, but for now, you need to be willing to be a rebel if you want to change.

If you asked 100 people from all over the world to tell you about their favorite foods, there would be many answers. Food preferences are mostly learned. Indeed, research suggests that infants learn about the types of foods eaten by their mothers during pregnancy and lactation and that these experiences bias us toward particular flavors and may program later food preferences. This is the first way (but not the only way) in which culture-specific food preferences are likely initiated early in life.

"The preference for energy- and fat-rich dishes is also shaped by the social context. Children often like foods they have eaten in pleasant situations and reject dishes linked to something negative. This is further enhanced by the selection of foods for specific occasions. Tasty foods (high-energy density, high-fat, and sugar content; e.g., desserts) are commonly served on pleasant occasions such as celebrations or when guests are visiting. In contrast, foods considered less tasty (e.g., vegetables) are often consumed under pressure: 'Eat your veggies or you won't get any dessert.' This results in doubly negative coupling and at the same time increases the popularity of energy-dense, tasty dishes and the aversion against less savory foods (Mennella, J. A. 2006).

This means that only foods or drinks are liked which one consumes on a regular basis and which therefore have become an acquired taste. If you practice eating healthy foods, you will learn to like them."

Practice the 10 Times and Mix It in Strategies

If you decide you want to learn to like a particular food like broccoli, eat it 10 times. If you still can't stand it, mix the broccoli with something you do like. Add sugar to it (remarkably tasty), or stir it into a dish you do like—mashed potatoes, for instance. You decide how much broccoli to add to the potatoes. As long as you can still taste some of the broccoli, you are creating an association between the broccoli taste with and something you like, and that is how you will learn to like it.

There are countless resources for healthy food recipes, so many that it can be overwhelming. Take things one step and one meal at a time, and try one new recipe. If you are interested in cooking, take an online cooking class to learn some new techniques.

Look up so recipes for side dishes that you have enjoyed in the past and modify them by reducing or even removing the oil and substituting water, broth, or wine. Don't expect things to change overnight. Be persistent, and one day you might like broccoli as much as you like mashed potatoes.

Be Vigilant

Successful lifetime weight management requires radar that is highly sensitive to moments of decision that determine if you will be powerful with food or not. If you have ever done obedience training with your dog, you know that you have to stay vigilant and continue to reinforce the rules. Your dog looks for opportunities to do what it wants, and if it senses that you will not be consistent about enforcing the rules, it will take advantage of that and start to misbehave.

Likewise, if you only realize that you have been eating poorly when your weight goes up a few days or weeks later, you missed the boat, and your alertness needs work. If you are at least aware of the fact that you are overeating while you are doing it, your watchfulness is in place, but you are waiting too long to act on it.

It is in a second that you make every decision that impacts your weight. You must develop your sensitivity to dangerous situations and practice taking immediate evasive action.

One of my favorite friends at my old weight-loss group told a story about how proud she was that she took an entire cake and threw it in the trash—at least for a few hours until she returned to the trash to dig it out. She learned that to truly get rid of something, she had to stuff it down the garbage disposal. I remember that story every time there is something tempting in the house.

Next time you are eating something you shouldn't, listen for the little voice that says:

"This is bad food. Put it down NOW!

"Stuff it down the sink where you can't get it. Quick!

"Get rid of this. Hurry!

Learn to listen to that voice and follow it. Because if you don't act right away, the next thought will be:

"Hmmm, this isn't bad. Maybe another bite."

Followed by: "I can start over tomorrow," or, "Just a few more bites won't hurt."

Without fail. If you hesitate, ignore that voice, and keep eating, you will find yourself in the very same situation again in a few hours or days. And if you keep eating, the scale will climb in a week or so, and you will remember why. It is because you did not act quickly enough when the little voice piped up.

As long as you encourage and listen to that voice, you will be successful. Every time it talks and you listen, pat yourself on the back. If it takes a few sentences for that good voice to break through, be patient and wait for it and then act on it. Learn to ignore the other voice. Let it trail off, or better yet, picture squashing it under your shoe.

CHANGE YOUR THOUGHTS

You must change your behavior with food if you want to control your weight. You can either fight it by relying on willpower (akin to holding your nose and swallowing your medicine), or you can decide to enjoy the behavior that will keep you lean. It all starts with a decision. Decide that you will

> learn to like healthy foods;

> enjoy the process of being vigilant about what you eat;

> diminish the importance of food in your life;

> focus less on certain tastes and textures (fat and sweets);

> connect happy emotions with refusing food (or better yet, with throwing it away);

> connect negative emotions with food pushers—people that want to control what you eat;

> be suspicious of the food industry that creates hyper-addictive food without regard for health consequences;

> act as if you love healthy foods and act as if you hate fast food;

> dress yourself in sturdy armor and don't acknowledge it when your mouth waters at the smell of a juicy hamburger;

> disassociate from food victims that suffer and whine about how unfair it all is; and

> focus only on the negatives of junk food.

Keep reminding yourself that the more you practice all this, the better you will get at it. As long as you keep practicing, you don't have to go back and live the truths in the black box.

These mental gymnastics are difficult at first, but soon you will get the hang of them, and each day you avoid the black box is a reward in itself. In a few weeks, you will actually start to feel differently about your weight-loss efforts, and you will begin to see results.

Eventually everything about weight control will get much, much easier. If you are persistent, you will have successfully rewired your brain at about the same time as you reach your goal weight. And then what? Don't change anything. This is your new way of life. You have arrived.

Make Yourself Mentally Strong

When you truly believe all of these things, weight management will be pretty easy. If you practice telling yourself these things on a regular basis, you will start to believe them, especially when you see how powerful these beliefs are and how much easier they make things. Yes, I am telling you to brainwash yourself, but you are doing it so that you can make lasting change for the better. The first and most important thing you need to drill into your head is this statement:

"Rewiring my brain is more important than anything in my quest for lifetime weight control."

When you are mentally strong, when you are unstoppable, all of the following statements will be true. For now, just pretend they are true by repeating them to yourself often.

1. It is easy for me to drive through a fast-food takeout window without buying anything for myself.
2. When I see a (hamburger/dessert/(fill in the blank_____)), I remember the truths in my black box, and I know that eating those things will prolong my suffering.
3. Nothing will prevent me from reaching my weight-loss goal. I am the supreme master of what I eat.
4. The best tasting bites of anything are the first few. As soon as I have eaten the best bites of an unhealthy food, it is easy to get rid of the rest.
5. When I realize I am eating a food that is bad for me, I throw it down the garbage disposal so I am done with it. This makes me feel so strong!
6. I love being in control of what I eat and how I think about food.
7. I am going to reach my goal weight and hold it happily for the rest of my life.
8. I am teaching myself to enjoy healthy food and to shy away from bad food.
9. Every time I say "no thanks" I feel more powerful.
10. I will never return to the black box again.
11. There is no way I will give up or give in.
12. There is no way I will allow someone else to decide what I eat.
13. Reaching my goal weight now is more important than:
    a. Convenience
    b. Going along with the crowd
    c. Being 100% comfortable all the time
    d. The taste of any food
    e. Avoiding hunger
    f. (fill in the blank_____)
14. Every morning I wake up stronger and leaner than the day before.
15. It is exciting to see my body transform.
16. I relish the feeling of hunger because I know when I am hungry, I am making progress.
17. I can't wait to see how much faster I will be at my goal weight.

I am happy with myself now that I am making progress with my weight.

I feel calm and in control of my eating.

I think like an athlete with everything I do.

> I never eat unhealthy foods with abandon.

> I don't linger on thoughts about how good any particular food will taste.

> I will never struggle with weight again.

> It doesn't matter what happens. Nothing will keep me from succeeding this time, right now, today.

> I am succeeding now because I am no longer making excuses.

> I know precisely what to do if I get off track.

Reading this list once is not enough. Choose a few statements that ring true and remind yourself of them several times a day. Bathe your mind in them. Post them on social media. Post them on your refrigerator, in your calendar, in your car, and at your desk. Email them to yourself. Tell yourself these things again and again and again. Live them. Be them. Soon they will be your truths, and when they are, your weight problems will be gone forever.

CHAPTER 8:
RULES FOR SUCCESS

Do not reward yourself with food. You are not a dog.

Stick closely to these rules during your weight-loss phase. In time, you will determine which ones work and which ones don't, and you can shorten the list. Most dieters stray from the rules too soon before they have taken hold, and this is one of the reasons why the weight returns. First, achieve your goal weight and hold it steady for six weeks.

RULE 1: PLAN AHEAD

Create a Recovery Plan for Slip-Ups

The most common question I hear is, "How do I get back on track after I go off my plan?"

Sometimes this happens slowly over time, but usually the setback is obvious at the moment it occurs. There is no doubt that you will get derailed a few times. Be ready for it. Be ready to find a moment of strength and immediately act on it. Think and act.

Here are some specific ways to do that:

1. Remember the black box and the horrors it contains and say out loud "Never again." Then imagine throwing the junk food that you are eating in the garbage disposal—seize that moment and actually do it, right then and there. Start running the water and shove the food out of your life and down into the garbage disposal. This is fast, drastic action to save yourself. It sounds dramatic, but it happens in an instant, and suddenly you are a superhero as the feeling of power and ultimate control washes over you.

2. Think and act. As soon as you realize what you are doing—that are you eating something you should not eat, or you are eating too much of something—physically distance yourself from it. Back away from the table, or run out the front door! Do something big and physical to R-E-M-O-V-E yourself. Once you are away, take a few moments and rethink things—do you really want to go back to the truths in the black box?

3. Think and act. Immediately start eating something else that is healthy while you still have the "bad" food in your mouth. This interrupts the pleasure of the taste and texture of the bad food.

4. If you have been off track for days or weeks, think and act. Pull your head out of the sand. Go step on the scale right now. Shake yourself up.

5. Think and act. Visit your friend the black box. Physically go to the box and open it up and start reading all the ugliness there again. When you start to feel the emotion in your gut (this may happen just at the thought of the black box), then change your physical environment. Remove all temptations from your house. Go to the store or a restaurant and buy three or four of your favorite healthy foods to take home with

you. Go out and do a cleansing, calorie-burning run that is at least an hour long. You don't have to run fast, and you can take walk breaks every 3 minutes or so.

6.   Think and act. Hit the refresh button on your environment. This helps to refresh you mentally. Clean up your environment—your room, your car, your office or workspace. Put something new in your space or move some furniture around—even if it is a minor change, you need to get your thoughts out of the denial or self-loathing or whatever place your thoughts are that are allowing you to act this way. The easiest way to do this is to change your environment or remove yourself from it.

Plan for this kind of slip-up by writing out an action plan. Revisit what motivated you to start this weight-loss project in the first place. Starting the plan took plenty of motivation, and you had it then, so retrace your steps to find it now.

Do not beat yourself up for having the momentary lapse; rather, congratulate yourself for nipping it in the bud and revel in the power it gives you to have terminated the eating. Remember that victory and replay it in your mind again and again.

Plan a Weekly Indulgence

If you are really missing a particular food, you can still have it if you plan for it. Decide what you miss most, then under-eat for a day or so to save up for the extra calories. Eat precisely the thing you crave most. If you settle for a substitute, you will probably end up eating several different (bad) things in your search to find satisfaction. Don't settle for a substitute! Enjoy the food, track the calories, get rid of the leftovers, and then return to your plan.

RULE 2: TRACK YOUR FOOD

It doesn't matter which method you use, you still should record what and how much you eat. If you don't at least record what you eat, you will have difficulty figuring out where you are going wrong if you aren't losing weight.

Recording your food intake requires some organization. At home, have a pad in the kitchen and write things down immediately. Use your fitness device, computer, email, cell phone, or a small notebook to keep track. You can also add a food list to your training log. The more detailed your list, the more helpful it will be. Tracking goes hand in hand with measuring the amount you are eating. In time, you can back away from the measuring, but the tracking will remain a task that you will rely upon and eventually return to throughout your life.

Something about writing the food down makes it more real and forces you to be conscious of what you are eating. Once you are in your stabilizing phase, often just a half day of tracking is enough to get you back to eating well after a little slip.

The exception to this rule is during actual workouts when you don't have to worry about tracking.

Weigh and Measure

Most of us underestimate the amount we eat. If you are going to closely track your calories, you also have to be precise about the amount you are eating. That means you have to measure and weigh as needed. If you don't already have them, invest in some dry measuring cups, liquid measuring cups, and a food scale that lists both grams and ounces. You can save time by measuring a bunch of servings all at once and storing them in single-serving sizes for later use.

At first you may be surprised by how tiny a single serving of food can be. This will make you appreciate the huge volumes of vegetables you can eat with abandon. Eating an entire bagged salad (with only one-third of the dressing that comes with it—measure and count the dressing) in one sitting is perfectly acceptable.

As you progress, you will get good at estimating amounts, but keep measuring everything until you hit your goal weight. After that you will transition to eyeballing it, but only as long as you can keep the weight off.

If your weight starts to go up, go back to weighing and measuring until it is down again.

RULE 3: WEIGH IN

Record Your Weight Daily During the Weight-Loss Phase

There is evidence that daily weighing helps you keep weight off. Staying off the scale is in vogue, but being on the scale is important for serious, committed weight controllers. Daily weighing has many advantages:

> The only way to become familiar with how much your weight fluctuates from day to day is to weigh yourself daily. It demonstrates the variability in your weight is based on what you eat, how you train, your monthly cycle, and your training load.

> Knowing the typical range of your weight fluctuations will help you distinguish a true weight gain from a temporary one. When you have achieved your lifelong weight, it is important to take action quickly when you put on a few pounds. Knowing your normal weight patterns will help you to recognize when you must act. Weighing daily will let you nip a weight gain in the bud so you can act on it when it is still tiny. It is also harder to deny a weight gain when it is staring you in the face day after day. Get into the habit now. It will help you in the future.

➤ You may see temporary weight gains following long training rides when you have consumed electrolytes and carbohydrates which tend to make you retain water. You may also see an increase after rigorous strength training sessions when you are sore. Some of this soreness is an inflammatory process in the muscles as they recover. These changes in the scale are not fat increases, so they should not alarm you.

➤ Weighing often (and recording your weight) will eventually dampen the emotional impact of an unexpected gain or loss. This is important because some people will see an unexpected weight loss as a cause for celebration and an invitation to slacken their food control for a few days. This can cause a weight gain. It is also important to overcome your emotional attachment to the scale. It is a tool that displays a number. How you manage the information is within your control. Taking control of your food includes taking control of your scale, too.

➤ Salty foods like soy sauce can raise your weight several pounds overnight. Consider what you have been eating. Remember that water comes and goes in a matter of hours. To gain a pound of fat requires overeating 3,500 calories. Do you really believe that your weight is up 4 pounds from yesterday because of the 700 calorie piece of cake you ate? Give your weight a few days to return to normal. Don't be a weight alarmist.

➤ The other scenario is getting overly discouraged by unexpected weight gain and turning to food for comfort. Being used to weight fluctuations will keep you away from food as a form of celebration or stress relief. This is a bad idea either way.

➤ Knowing your weight keeps you honest. Even if you do not eat excess calories and gain weight, what you put into your body has an immediate impact on the scale. Sometimes it is helpful to weigh more than once a day. Before and after workouts will tell you about your sweat rate. If you have trouble remembering to do this, keep a scale in the garage next to your bike so you are reminded to record your weight before and after you ride.

➤ If you are trying to control after-dinner eating, weighing several times a day may help. A 2004 study had people record their weight four times a day. The people that were significantly heavier before bedtime were more likely to gain weight than the ones whose weight remained stable throughout the day (National Weight Control Registry, 2009).

Weekly Accountability

In this context, accountability is officially weighing in on a weekly basis and reporting the result to someone else. Doing so forces you to accept the choices you made that week and to move forward to the next one with a clean slate. The threat of embarrassment is added motivation.

Accountability is also encouraged in commercial weight management programs that include regular cell phone, text message, or email contact with a counselor. These programs that incorporate weight-related support along with regular contact have been quite effective.

RULE 4: LIMIT FOOD CHOICES

Stop Sampling

When you go to the local grocery store, the lunchtime sample tables are everywhere, and, for many, the samples provided accumulate into a free meal. Perhaps they are free in terms of money, but they are certainly not free in terms of calories. You should get out of the habit of eating simply because food is free and available. If you let the environment decide on your diet, you are doomed. Those little nibbles add up quickly. Don't even start. Just walk away. You can do it.

Another source of sampling temptation is with your kids. Stop sampling your kid's French fries. Stop taking a spoonful of their ice cream or a bite of birthday cake. Say, no thanks.

Skip the Buffet

Novel foods stimulate the reward pathways in the brain that tell you to eat even if you are not hungry. In other words, you eat more where there are lots of yummy choices. This is one reason people eat more food at a restaurant buffet then when they are at home.

With this in mind, if you want to eat more of a certain kind of food, you should have a large variety of it around. Most athletes will benefit from eating more vegetables, fruit, beans, lentils, and nuts. These foods are the cornerstone of good nutrition, superior performance, and controlling hunger. Since you will benefit from eating more LCD foods, you should have a variety of them available.

Likewise, you want to eat less HCD food, so you shouldn't tempt yourself. It is helpful to keep fewer of these foods around. Less variety means less temptation. People who successfully maintain weight loss eat a small variety of foods, especially the HCD kind.

RULE 5: AVOID ALCOHOL

There is controversy about some aspects of how alcohol consumption influences health. Alcohol is trouble for weight management because of the following:

1. Alcohol is more calorically dense than carbohydrate or protein. It is a HCD food.
2. It has virtually no nutritional value.
3. Alcohol suppresses the number of fat calories your body burns for energy, replacing fat as a source of fuel.
4. It stimulates hunger.
5. It impairs judgment, making it harder to stick to your food program.
6. Alcohol reduces testosterone levels, especially after exercise, which may explain why people who drink a lot of alcohol carry less muscle.

Strategies for reducing alcohol intake include:

> Limiting intake to one day per week

> Limiting the amount to one or two glasses

> Drinking a large glass of water before an alcoholic drink

> ➤ Adding ice, fresh fruit, carbonated water, and some fruit juice to red wine to make a bubbly sangria

> ➤ Keeping water next to you and drinking it between sips of alcohol

RULE 6: KEEP YOUR ENVIRONMENT SAFE

No Junk Food

It is easier to do battle with temptation in the grocery store than in your own house late at night when the food is calling to you. Do a quick check of your shopping cart before you pay. If you are embarrassed by any of the food in your cart, you should probably not be buying it. Listen to the voice in your head that is promising to avoid overeating the food you are buying. Don't put yourself through the temptation in the first place.

Have Access to Safe Snacks

Your home should be a safe and restful place. When you get hungry, you should be able to find healthy LCD foods to munch on. All it takes is planning. By keeping tempting,

poor-quality foods out of your house, you can keep that little junk food voice from calling your name. Instead, stock up on safe foods like fruits, vegetables, and air foods like air-popped corn.

You will also get hungry at work or in your car, so make those areas safe as well. Keep a cooler in your car stocked with bulky LCD food. If you can remember to keep an ice block in your cooler, you will have even more options. Bringing your own lunch is the best way to control what you eat.

Having food in your car will also keep you from seeking fast food out of hunger. A growing variety of pre-cooked foods that do not require refrigeration are available. Seek those out, and keep some staples like almonds and raisins on hand, too.

Along the same lines, don't bring HCD junk foods into your house or your workplace.

Do not fall victim to the excuse of buying junk for the kids, for my husband, or for the gang at work. You are not fooling anyone but yourself. Create an environment that guarantees success.

Throw Out Unhealthy Food

Believe it or not, throwing food out is an important and, for some, difficult skill. Our reluctance to waste food comes mostly from family history and cultural norms. In some people, the little voice inside scolds them about wasting food. It is up to you how to argue with that voice, but on a practical level, you don't want to do anything that offends someone you care about. Don't launch your aunt's cheesecake into the bin in front of her face. Wait until she is gone. Be polite, be discrete, but get rid of the cake before it becomes a temptation.

When you are alone and you start to hear a food calling to you, take control. Throw it away. Sometimes the trash can is not enough, so put it down the sink.

The choice is pretty clear. Either you remove the food from your environment, or you will eventually eat in and wear it on your thighs or your gut. You can shortcut the process by attaching the offending food to your skin directly with some duct tape.

Getting rid of junk food has another perk: It makes you feel powerful.

Don't worry about the financial impact. Eating food you don't want to eat, putting on weight, and suffering the emotional pain of a weight problem are more costly than the food you toss out.

RULE 7: FOCUS ON EMPOWERMENT

Pay Attention to Success

Every bit of progress should be acknowledged. Define progress as behavior that moves you toward controlling your weight. It can be making a good choice, throwing away a half-eaten cake that has been tempting you, or foregoing your usual soda for water. You need not throw a party, but mentally add another victory to your list and be strengthened by it.

In addition to tracking what you eat, you should track your victories, too. Make a list of the foods you could have eaten (would have eaten if you had not decided to change your life) and that you did not eat (figure 30). Each one of these moments of resistance is a positive step, and you have probably never before kept track of them. Now is the time to start.

Fig. 30 Food victory list

Food Victories for Today

Renew Motivation

Renew your motivation every day. Imagine your life at your new weight. See yourself making the right decisions to get you there. Go ahead and plan on success. Get the new racing outfit that you will fit into. Behave as if achieving your goal is a foregone conclusion. Make it who you are.

Start expanding your world. You may not realize that there are all sorts of things you have probably avoided doing because you are self-conscious about your weight. What will you do once you are free of that burden? Are there people you will see that you avoided before? Are there races in exotic locations that you could use to celebrate your victory? Are there different kinds of clothes that you have avoided but that you will wear now?

Invest in the best looking, most flattering workout clothes you can afford. Your triathlon-run-gym clothes are the ones that should make you feel your best.

Say No to Just One Bite

Saying no to food in social settings can be a dicey proposition, depending on who is offering the food and how they expect you to react. There is no reason that an adult should have to eat, even just a bite of something they don't want. Saying "no thank you" is a polite response, and it should end the matter, but often it doesn't work that way.

Relinquishing control of what you eat to anyone else is a bad idea. What do you think it means to be in control of your food? It means that you call the shots, every day, all day.

The person offering you the food does not realize that even one bite of something has a psychological and chemical consequence. A taste of sugar can set in motion a craving for the stuff that you will have to battle the rest of the day—all because of one little bite.

You should become familiar with particular foods that can trigger your appetite. For some, it is salty crunchy chips; for others, it is sweets; and still for others it is starches. Although, calorically speaking, you need not eliminate any particular food to lose weight, you should stay away from foods that set into motion an intense desire for more.

Family politics are up to you to manage. If food is offered and you can't refuse without someone causing a scene, take it, but don't eat it. When you can, throw it in the trash, the yard, or just leave it with the dirty dishes.

A single bite of something can trigger a craving; it can provide 100 or more unwanted calories; and worst of all, you are putting someone else is in control of your eating, which is a bad thing.

RULE 8: USE TIME TO YOUR ADVANTAGE

1. Limit holiday overeating to a select few meals rather than to an entire season. Decide ahead of time which occasions are the most tempting, then limit the number of hours of indulgence.

2. Limit your time exposure to tempting, unhealthy foods by getting rid of the leftovers as soon as your planned (or unplanned) indulgence is over. It goes without saying that you should not take junk food leftovers home, ever. If for some reason you do, dispose of the food as soon as you can.

3. Set a time limit when you find yourself eating the wrong food. The shorter the time limit, the less damage will be done, and the sooner you can get back on track. Be sure to celebrate your successful return to your plan. Returning to the plan quickly is a much more significant event than the fact that you strayed off the plan.

4. Set a rest interval when you are eating. This interval eating can be effective anytime. Eat a few bites, and then put your fork down for up to a minute. At some point, you will be ready to move on to another activity.

5. Another way to limit time exposure to junk food is to eat it outside of the home. If you have to go out for a scoop of ice cream, you will not be tempted to go back again and again as you would if the stuff was in your refrigerator.

RULE 9: GET RID OF THINGS THAT DON'T FIT ANYMORE

Get Rid of Clothes That Are Too Small

Let go of the past. There is no reason to keep those skinny jeans in the back of your closet or any other clothing that has not fit you for a while. There is nothing encouraging or motivating about a pile of clothes that you used to be able to wear that are now too tight.

It is important to realize that clothing is a product manufactured by a machine according to a pattern that either closely matches your shape or it does not. The manufacturing process can be precise, in which case the end product matches the pattern used, or it can be sloppy (or with cheap fabrics that don't hold their shape). In either case, poorly made garments lack uniformity from piece to piece, even if they are the same size. An article of clothing is not a judgment of whether your body is the "correct" size or shape.

So finding something that fits you perfectly is more a matter of luck than a matter of you being lean enough.

I remember putting on pants that were too tight, looking in the mirror, and wishing my thighs or belly were smaller so the pants would fit right. I used the fit of the pants to point out areas where I was too fat and the ways in which I did not confirm to "normal" or to the "ideal."

Years later after losing 60 pounds, it is still difficult to find pants that fit right, even in a small size! The waist is still gaping while the thighs are a bit snug. I finally realized that it wasn't about me being "right," it was about the pants being "right for me." Now I recognize that it is the job of the pants to fit me. If they don't fit, they fail to do their job, and there is no sense keeping them. I haven't put on a tight pair of pants for years. As soon as I feel that they are too hard to pull over my rear, off they go. Life is too short to waste money on the wrong clothes. Just the thought of pulling on a pair to too-tight pants and struggling to zip them makes me anxious.

How about triathlon clothes? The main areas of difficulty are the leg openings which are often too tight, giving you "sausage legs," low-cut shorts that create a muffin top or gut overspill, tri tops that are too short (see muffin top and gut overhang), arm openings that are too small, forming a "pitflap" in the front and a "backflap" in the back. Really, the bigger concern should be comfort, but it is possible to find better-fitting race and training clothes if you are willing to shop around. If you order a bunch of styles all at once online, you can try them on at home and return the ones that don't work.

Whether it is tri clothing or street clothes, please do not use clothing to judge you.

Get Rid of Clothes That Are Too Large

You will be getting smaller as you achieve weight management success. Will you hold on to the clothing that gets too big, or will you keep it as a safety net just in case you put the weight back on? This one is easy. Since you have decided that you will not be putting the weight back on, and since you are the only one who can control your weight, you have no reason to keep those too-big clothes around. Keeping them around undermines your decision to stay lean for life. The way you are eating when you are losing weight is the new normal. You must behave as if that is true. Get rid of clothing that is too big for you right away.

The one exception is that you can keep one piece of clothing that you wore at your largest as a remembrance. It is motivating to go back and hold up that pair of pants or that giant shirt and to acknowledge how dramatically you have changed.

RULE 10: GATHER PERSONAL SUPPORT

The most powerful tool you have in social situations is your attitude. If you exude certainty about the outcome of your weight-loss program, others will accept it. If you express doubt, others will exploit it. Comments from people you care about have an impact. If your attitude is based on the belief that you will not fail, comments will not weaken your resolve. Seek support of your strongest self.

Losing weight will be easier if the immediate family supports your effort.

The main objection family members have to your weight-loss plan is the change in meals and foods available to them. Eating better should not cause a ruckus in the household. You don't have to go crazy and strip the house of foods the rest of your family enjoys. Be smart and limit the foods that tempt you. Use the skills from chapter 7 and keep eating normal food. After a few days, the family will get on board.

When it comes to coworkers and extended family, it is often best to keep your efforts to yourself and let them see the results over time. Making a big deal over your new food plan will put the focus and pressure on you. They won't know what food to offer you.

Announcing your intentions also creates pressure in your own psyche. It is really no one's business what you eat, and the less you call attention to it, the more natural it will be for you. Your new way of eating is not temporary; it is a new reality that will stay with you for the rest of your life.

Another avenue of support is what you read. There are plenty of inspiring books about weight loss that will help you feel less alone in your quest.

Suggested Reading:

> The End of Overeating by David A. Kessler, MD (Rodale, 2009).

> The 9 Truths About Weight Loss by Daniel S. Kirschenbaum, PhD (Henry Holt, 2000).

> Heft on Wheels by Mike Magnuson (Harmony, 2004).

> Till We Eat Again: Confessions of a Diet Dropout by Judy Gruen (Champion, 2002).

> Slow Fat Triathlete by Jayne Williams (Da Capo, 2004).

Structured Weight-Loss Groups

Structured weight-loss programs that incorporate behavioral treatment diet change and encourage physical activity improve your psychological state and your mood. Support can be one on one or in groups. Contrast this with the many freeform chat rooms online. These forums might be helpful, but too often they are full of people that tend to whine and complain about their struggles. See if you can find one that focuses on successful weight loss and taking control of your weight. The group should motivate you to be better rather than console you for making excuses.

Men aren't usually comfortable at traditional weight-support meetings, but there are alternatives. With the Internet and cell phones, online- or phone-supported weight-loss programs are widely available. WeightWatchers®, which I highly recommend, has group support and online support and an online program especially for men.

The idea of traditional group support may be unappealing because as an athlete you think you will not have much in common with the mostly older women you see at a typical WeightWatchers® meeting. This perception is correct to some degree, but on the other hand, food issues are food issues, no matter who has them. You may be surprised by how much you have in common with those women when it comes to food. Your athleticism obviously puts you way ahead of the game when it comes to exercise, but just imagine how helpful your comments will be. Give it a try, and you will be pleasantly surprised by how much positive information is available at group support meetings.

CHAPTER 9:
FUEL YOUR TRAINING

HOW TO BE A SAINT ON THE COUCH AND A SINNER ON THE BIKE

How do you do fuel your training and lose weight at the same time? It is very difficult. Weight loss is the first priority now. Your performance might suffer, so put it on the backburner until you have reached your goal weight. It's that simple.

We know that in the past you have relied too much on training as a safety net to overeating. In my experience, the best way to change this and to be able to continue training is to do the following:

1. Stick to eating (counting and recording) your baseline number of calories at all times except when you are actually doing a workout or eating your recovery meal. This is important because you need to be able to control your weight even if you aren't training at all. This is the part about being a saint on the couch (see figure 31).

2. Fuel adequately during your workouts (more on this later). Do not count the calories you consume during workout against the baseline limit. The calories you eat during a workout are fuel for the workout, but these are free calories and this is your chance to eat sugary foods since this is when you actually need them. This is when you can be a sinner on the bike.

3. Eat an adequate recovery meal after longer workouts. Like the fuel you take in during your workouts, these recovery meals are not counted in your daily calories. These meals are meant to replenish the glycogen stores in your muscles and nothing more. By eating soon after your workouts, you are assured that the calories are going directly (more or less) into your muscles, where they are needed most.

4. After your recovery meal, go back to eating according to your baseline calorie limit.

Fig. 31 Saint on the couch and a sinner on the bike plan

Breakfast	During workout	Post workout	Lunch	Dinner	Snacks
Calories count toward daily baseline	100 calories every 30 min.	100 calories for every 60 min.	Calories count toward daily baseline	Calories count toward daily baseline	Calories count toward daily baseline

Baseline Calories

Use an online calculator to determine your daily calorie needs based on a low activity level—what you do at work and during your non-training time. So if you walk your dog every day, for example, you can include that in your baseline activity. But don't include any of your true workouts. This will give you a baseline calorie expenditure, excluding workouts. It is an important number, and one you should record in your weight management plan. There will come a time when you aren't training, and knowing that you know how to eat to stay lean even without it is an important skill. It is also a real confidence builder.

So work through the calculator using a low activity level and see what your calorie needs are to lose weight at a rate of .5 to 1 pound per week. That is your baseline calorie intake.

You can stop here if you plan to use the saint on the couch and a sinner on the bike program.

If you prefer to count all of your calories, everything you eat at all times, including during workouts and recovery meals, you are free to do so. It is a bit of a hassle because you have to know exactly how many ounces of fuel you drank and account for any that you left in the bottle. Precision is key. It is interesting to play with the numbers, though. This should show an increased calorie level based on your current training level. It is perfectly fine to eat according to that calorie level, but by doing so, you are not teaching yourself to separate training-related eating from normal activity eating.

HOW TO FUEL FOR WORKOUTS AND RACES

Here are the fueling guidelines, starting from before a race or workout to the recovery afterward. These apply for short-course and long-course athletes.

➤ Don't carbo load.

➤ Eat a few hours before you train; count those calories.

➤ Eat a sugary snack 30 minutes before a short race or short, intense workout (optional); count those calories.

➤ Refuel with sugar during workouts—free calories.

➤ Start fueling after 30 minutes—free calories.

➤ Consume 200 calories per hour during workouts—free calories.

➤ Caffeine helps.

➤ Be careful with salt.

➤ Reload right after your session with 100 calories for every 30 minutes of workout time.

Don't Carbo Load

Carbo loading is designed to load your liver and muscles with extra glycogen, but it doesn't work that way. Your liver and muscles can only absorb a finite amount, and when you overload, it just makes you fatter and slower on race day. It works better to eat normally, but ease off on training in the three days before your race.

Eat Before Your Workout

If you eat too close to your workout session, your stomach will still be full, and your digestion will slow down when you start to exercise. You will not have gotten all the value out of your food, and you will be uncomfortable.

It is best to eat a high-carbohydrate meal (several hundred calories) about three hours before your long sessions. This gives your system time to absorb the calories. If, for some reason, you train on an empty stomach, you will have to begin refueling right away rather than waiting the usual 90 minutes, and it will be especially critical to reload after the workout. This meal will probably be breakfast, and you should count these calories against your baseline.

Eat or drink something sweet like a gel, drink, or candy within 30 minutes before exercising for improved performance early in a short, intense workout or if you are doing a sprint or Olympic distance race. Count these calories, too.

Fuel With Sugar During Workouts

At rest, you burn mostly fat. If you are training, you burn mostly sugar (in the form of glucose). Daily activities burn a combination of both.

The speed your muscles are able to work in endurance exercise depends entirely on how fast blood can move oxygen into your muscles. Sugar allows oxygen to get into muscles faster than fat and protein. That is why sugar will allow you to move the fastest in endurance events. Think of sugar as speedboat rushing oxygen into your muscles.

Your muscles take sugar first from the blood, then from liver stores that are released into the bloodstream. When the liver is empty, it uses sugar stored in the muscles. The aim in fueling as you train is to conserve those sugar stores in the liver and, ultimately, the stores in the muscles.

Taking in sugar every 15 minutes prevents your glycogen and sugar stores from getting too low. This allows you to keep moving fast.

The number of calories you take in depends on your tolerance, but most people can handle 200 calories per hour, so 50 calories every 15 minutes or 100 calories every 30 minutes. More than that can cause stomach upset and slow gastric emptying.

For athletes who are not trying to lose weight, the timing of sugar intake depends on how long your race or training session is. For this program, the formula is simple: 100 calories every 30 minutes. You can take it in two small doses, one every 15 minutes, or you can do it all at once at 30 minutes.

If you do not take in sugar, you will bonk or hit the wall from low blood sugar about 90 minutes into workout. If your brain (which also runs on sugar) runs out of fuel, you can faint, feel confused, or have convulsions. Your muscles have to get oxygen from fat rather than sugar, and this is a s-l-o-w process. You will still be able to move forward, but you will continue to move very slowly, no matter how hard you try to speed up or how well-trained you are. Your muscles will work very slowly, too—so slowly that you are no longer getting a training benefit, and you are certainly not racing as much as surviving.

Bonking in cycling races are more dramatic than those in running because the legs can empty their stores faster than in long-distance running. This is because running damages muscles so much that the runner has to slow down because of the damage before they get to the point of using all their fuel. When the runner slows, he uses fuel less quickly and can stay ahead of depletion more easily by taking in fuel. (See www.dr.mirkin.com)

Cortisol, a stress hormone, is also released when your glycogen stores get low. One of the things cortisol does is to protect glycogen stores so that you don't use protein (your muscles) for fuel. Fueling properly during your workouts keeps cortisol levels down, ultimately protecting the muscles.

Can you enhance performance by restricting sugar during training and thus teaching the muscles to get along with less sugar? There is some evidence that training this way on occasion induces some adaptations that could have some benefit, but that is still up for debate. At this point, it is certain that you will recover faster and be able to train harder if your muscles are well fueled.

WHAT TO EAT

Solids vs. Liquids

Once in the gut, liquids are processed more easily than solids. In order of ease of digestion, while training you should consume sports drink, gel with water chaser, soft candies, and then solids. Solid food certainly provides a better sense of satisfaction, though, so on your long training days you should give it a try during long, lower intensity sessions. Look at The Feed Zone Portables: A Cookbook of On-the-Go Food for Athletes by Allen Lim and Biju Thomas (VeloPress, 2013) for suggestions.

As a practical matter, getting solid food down while in the aero position can be difficult, so you have to experiment. A periodic, 60-second stop and stretch break at the end of each hour of ride time can work wonders to stave off muscle fatigue, especially when holding the aero position on a flat course for many hours. These breaks are a great time to wolf down some extra food.

Protein

Taking in some protein during long efforts (over 2.5 hours) may have some benefits, but that is not conclusive. Protein can interfere with gastric emptying, so be careful if you tend to suffer from gastrointestinal issues. There is no indication that protein causes harm during a workout, so it is really up to you whether to include it in your fueling strategy.

Caffeine

Caffeine increases endurance during long events by helping muscles use more sugar. Caffeine increases the entry of sugar into muscles by as much as 26 percent. It also helps athletes run faster in both short- and long-distance races. Be careful if you are sensitive to caffeine. The last thing you need is to lose sleep because you took in too much caffeine during your workout. Try using it late in your workout on your longest training days and, of course, on race day.

Salt

The use of salt supplementation during endurance events has changed over time. At one time, salt was supposed to have a role in muscle cramping. That has been refuted. Then researchers concerned themselves with replacing the salt lost during long and hot races. It turned out that the sodium levels in Ironman finishers didn't differ much between athletes who were heavy sweaters and those who did not sweat as much, and that low sodium levels are rare. The role of salt as an aid in keeping the body cool (thermoregulation) has also been studied, and no conclusive benefit was found.

Recently, the role of salt in aiding transport of water out of the gut to keep an athlete hydrated is the focus. Products like Osmo, Skratch, and The Right Stuff are being marketed to endurance athletes. Anecdotally, these products indeed make some athletes feel better during long races and training sessions, but the science to back that up a real benefit is far from conclusive. The science that is referenced on the websites of these products is mostly outdated.

A recent review of this topic appeared in the Journal of Sports Science and Medicine (March 2015) in the article "Effects of oral sodium supplementation on indices of thermoregulation in trained, endurance athletes," sums it up nicely:

Based on current professional recommendations to replace sodium losses in sweat during exercise, some endurance athletes consume salt or other electrolyte supplements containing sodium during training and competition, however the effects of sodium on thermoregulation are less clear. High-dose sodium supplementation does not appear to impact thermoregulation, cardiovascular drift, or physical performance in trained, endurance athletes. The possibility remains that high sodium intakes might have other adverse effects. It is our recommendation that athletes interpret professional recommendations for sodium needs during exercise with caution (Earhart, Weiss, Rahman et al., 2015, p. 172).

Bottom line: Be cautious with salt.

RELOAD, DON'T OVERLOAD

Most athletes have heard about a two-hour post-workout window during which the muscles are superabsorbent for glycogen. This is true, but the effect actually lasts up to nine hours, and it is strongest immediately after your workout before tapering off. If, for some reason, you don't get your recovery meal in within the two hours, your muscles will still refill just fine in time for tomorrow's session. The short time window is important only for athletes who will have another workout within the next eight hours.

Include 20 grams (80 calories) of protein to rebuild damaged muscle after long or hard workouts. Portable plant source suggestions include: pumpkin seeds, cashews, and hummus. There is no benefit to eating extra protein. It will not make you recover faster or grow stronger. It mostly makes your kidneys work harder. You are better off focusing on replenishing carbohydrates after a long session.

The size of the recovery meal should reflect the size of your workout. Use the simple 100 rule (figure 32) as a guideline. "Reload, don't overload" is one of the rules you should start to live by in the weight-loss phase of your program.

Calorie needs are higher for harder workouts that are done at a higher heart rate (HR). The calorie ranges will cover athletes of various sizes. It goes without saying that if you are a small female, you should choose the lower calorie range than a large male who should be at the upper end. You don't have to weigh and measure every ounce of your recovery meal. They are part of your free calories. So, yes, it matters that you don't overdo, but you will be making adjustments as you go. If you don't lose any weight in the first week, eat a smaller recovery meal. Likewise, if you lose more than 2 pounds per week for four weeks in a row, eat a slightly larger recovery meal. You want to slow your rate of weight loss just a little, not stop it altogether.

Fig. 32 Simple 100 rule—Fueling guidelines for workouts and races

Eat during workout	100 calories every 30 min. Start at 30 min.
Post-workout recovery meal	100 calories for every hour of training.

But I'm Training for an Ironman!

If you are training for an Ironman, you might be surprised how little those longer hours buy you in terms of extra calories.

A typical 24-week training program has a four-week cycle; three weeks of increasing volume is followed by one week of reduced volume (3-up, 1-down cycle). Starting with base of 10 hours per week, training volume increases by about an hour a week. In any four-week cycle, the training volume increases, on average, about two hours per week. The athlete will eventually build to about 20 hours but will only have a few weeks at that level. Volumes then decrease into the taper.

If the athlete follows this standard training plan, the volume increases so slowly that by race day, the average training volume for the week is only five hours over base level. The athlete goes from a 10-hour average to a 15-hour average. Aside from a few very long days in the saddle, this does not justify a huge or prolonged increase in calorie intake.

Increasing average training volume by five hours per week for a 160-pound athlete using 600 calories per hour (an average calorie expenditure for Ironman paced training) increases calorie requirements by 3,000 calories per week (5 hr/wk x 600 cal/hr = 3,000 cal/wk).

That sounds like a lot, but don't forget that you are also consuming calories during most of those hours.

5 hours x 200 calories per hour = 1,000 additional calories consumed, so now that extra 3,000 calories you need is reduced to 2,000. This comes out to 286 extra calories a day, enough for a modest recovery meal after training or a candy bar every day. That isn't much. Ironman training is not a license to eat everything in sight.

SOURCES

Abbot JM, Thomson CA, Ranger-Moore J, Teixeira PJ, et al. Psychosocial and behavioral profile and predictors of self-reported energy underreporting in obese middle-aged women. J Am Diet Assoc. 2008 Jan; 108 (1): 114-9.

Ackroff K, Bonacchi K, Magee M, Yiin YM, Graves J, Sclafani A. Obesity by choice revisited: Effects of food availability, flavor variety and nutrient composition on energy intake Physiol Behav. 2007 Oct 22; 92 (3): 468-78. Epub 2007 Apr 24.

America's general approval of cosmetic surgery. American Society for Aesthetic Plastic Surgery 2008. www.surgery.org

Annu Rev Nutr. 2009 Apr 27. Epub ahead of print.

Aragon, A. A., & Schoenfeld, B. J. (2013). Nutrient timing revisited: is there a post-exercise anabolic window? Journal of the International Society of Sports Nutrition, 10, 5. http://doi.org/10.1186/1550-2783-10-5

Arrese AL, Ostariz ES, Skinfold thicknesses associated with running performance in highly trained runners. J Sport Sci 2006; 24: 69-76.

Bale P, Rowell S, Colley E. Anthropometric and training characteristics of female marathon runners as determinants of distance running performance. J Sports Sci 1985 3: 115-126.

Ballor DL, Katch VL, Becque MD, Marks CR, Resistance weight training during caloric restriction enhances lean body weight maintenance. American Journal of Clinical Nutrition. 1988, 47 (1): 19-25.

Ballor DL, Poehlman ET,. Exercise-training enhances fat-free mass preservation during diet-induced weight loss: a meta-analytical finding. Int J Obes Relat Metab Disord. 1994 Jan 18; (1): 35-40.

Bamber DJ, Cockerill IM, Rodgers S, Carroll D. Diagnostic criteria for exercise dependence in women. Br J Sports Med 2003;37: 393-400

Bassett DR, Kyle CR, Passfield L, Broker JP, Burke ER. Comparing cycling world hour records, 1967-1996: modeling with empirical data. Med Sci Sports Exerc 1999;31 (11): 1665-1676.

Bellisle F, Drewnowski A. Intense sweeteners, energy intake and the control of body weight. Euro J Clin Nutr. 2007 Jun; 61 (6): 691-700. Epub 2007 Feb 7.

Blaine BE, Rodman J, Newman JM: Weight loss treatment and psychological well-being: a review and meta-analysis. J Health Psychol 2007, 12: 66-82.

Boutcher, S. H. (2011). High-Intensity Intermittent Exercise and Fat Loss. Journal of Obesity, 2011, 868305. http://doi.org/10.1155/2011/868305

Browning RC, Modica JR, Kram R, Goswami A. The effects of adding mass to the legs on the energetics and biomechanics of walking. Med Sci. Sports Exerc 2007, 29: 515-525.

Bunc V, Heller J, Horcic J, Novotny J, Physiological profile of best Czech m

Burton P, Smith HJ, Lightowler HJ. The influence of restrained and external eating patters on overeating. Appetite. 2007 Jul; 49 (1): 191-197.

Butryn ML, Phelan S, Hill JO, Wing RR. Consistent self-monitoring of weight: a key component to successful weight loss maintenance. Obesity (Silver Spring). 2007 Dec; 15 (12): 3091-6.

Chatard JC, Padilla S, Cazorla G, Lacour R, Influence of body height, weight, hydrostatic lift and training on the energy cost of the front crawl. NZ Sports Med 1985;13: 82-84.

Collins MA, Millard-Stafford ML, Sparling PB, et al. Evaluation of the BOD POD for assessing body fat in collegiate football players, Med Sci Sports Exerc 1999 31 (9): 1350-1356.

Cook Gray. Athletic Body in Balance 2005, Human Kinetics, p. 9.

Cooling J, Blundell J. Are high-fat and low-fat consumers distinct phenotypes? Differences in the subjective and behavioral response to energy and nutrient challenges. Eur J Clin Nutr. 1998; 52 (3): 193-201.

Costill DL, Kovaleski J, Porter D, Kirwan J, Fielding R, King D. Energy expenditure during front crawl swimming: predicting success in middle-distance events.

De Castro JM. The effects of the spontaneous ingestion of particular foods or beverages on the meal patterns and overall nutrient intake of humans. Physiol. Behav. (1993) 53: 1133-1144.

Debate RD, Turner M, Flowers C, Wethington H. Eating attitudes, body image, and nutrient intake in female triathletes. 9/22/02, Women Sport Physl Act J.

Deibert P, Konig D, Vitolins MZ, et al, Effect of a weight loss intervention on anthropometric measure and metabolic risk factors in pre-versus post menopausal women. Nutr J. 2007; 6: 31.

Diagnostic and Statistical Manual of Mental Disorders, Fourth Edition. Copyright 1994 American Psychiatric Association

DiGioacchino DR, Wethington H, Sargent R.Body size dissatisfaction among male and female triathletes. Eating and Weight Disorders 2002 Sept, 7 (4): 316-323.

Earhart EL, Weiss EP, Rahman R, Kelly PV. (2015) Effects of Oral Sodium Supplementation on Indices of Thermoregulation in Trained, Endurance Athletes. Journal of Sports Science and Medicine (14), 172-178.

Fields DA, Higgins PB, Hunter GR. Assessment of body composition by air-displacement plethysomography: influence of body temperature and moisture. Dynamic Medicine, 2004.

Fitzgerald, Matt. Protein and the Endurance Athlete. Triathlete Magazine, January 27, 2015.

Forster JL, Jeffery RW. Gender differences related to weight history, eating patterns, efficacy expectations, self-esteem, and weight loss among participants in a weight reduction program. Addict Behav. 1986; 11 (2): 141-7.

Fuhrman J, Dr. See articles at www.drfuhrman.com.

Gilbert JA, Drapeau V, Astrup A, Tremblay A. Relationship between diet-induced changes in body fat and appetite sensations in women. Appetite. 2009 Jun; 52 (3): 809-12. Epub 2009 Apr 21.

Gordon MM, Bodd MJ, Ester L, et al. Effect of dietary protein on the composition of weight loss in post menopausal women. J Nutr Health Aging. 2008 Oct; 12 (8): 505-9.

Gruenfeld, L. from Beyond Beyond: The Next Unnatural Step. 9/28/08 Ironman.com.

Guerrieri R, Nederkoorn C, Jansen A. The interaction between impulsivity and a varied food environment: its influence on food intake and overweight. Int J Obes (Lond). 2008 Apr; 32 (4): 708-14. Epub 2007 Dec 4.

Haapala I, Barengo NC, Biggs S, Surakka L, Manninen P. Weight loss by mobile phone: a 1-year effectiveness study. Public Health Nutr. 2009 Mar 27: 1-10.

Hall et al., 2016. "Quantification of the effect of energy imbalance on bodyweight." Lancet, 378.9793 (2011): 10.1016/S0140−6736(11)60812−X. PMC. Web. 11 Feb. 2016.

Harris J, Benedict F. A biometric study of basal metabolism in man. Washington D.C. 1919 Carnegie Institute of Washington.

Health Statistics Plastic Surgery procedures (per capita) (most recent) by country. www.Nationmaster.com (retrieved 6/2009).

Heikkonen E, Ylikahri R, Roine R. Valimaki M, et al. The combined effect of alcohol and physical exercise on serum testosterone, leutenizing hormone, and cortisol in males. Alcoholism, Clinical and Experimental Research, 1996, 20, 711-716.

Hellemans I. Maximizing Olympic Distance Triathlon Performance: A Sports Dietitian's Perspective. Proceedings from the Gatorade International Triathlon Science II Conference, Noosa, AU, 11/7-11/8, 1999.

Heyward, VH. Evaluation of body composition. Current Issues. Sports Medicine, 1996 Sep; 22 (3): 146-56.

Hoch AZ, Stravakos JE, Schimke JE. Prevalence of female athlete triad characteristics in a club triathlon team. Arch Phys Med Rehabil. 2007 May; 88 (5): 681-2.

Holmér I. Oxygen uptake during swimming in man. J Appl Physiol. 1972 Oct; 33 (4): 502-9.

Int J Sports Med. 1985 Oct; 6 (5): 266-70.

Jackson AS, Ellis KJ, McFarlin BK, Sailors MH, Bray MS. Cross validation of generalized body composition equations with divers young men and women: the Training Intervention and Genetics of Exercise Response (TIGER) Study. Br J Nutr. 2009 Mar; 101 (6): 871-8. Epub 2008 Aug 15.

Jeukendrup A, Gleeson M. Sport Nutrition. 2004, Human Kinetics.

Kastor A, Salt Sugar Fat: Explore the Dark Side of the All-American Meal, America's Food Addiction, and Why We Get Fat. A&S Publishing, 2013.

Katch, Frank, Katch, Victor, McArdle, William. Exercise Physiology: Energy, Nutrition, and Human Performance, 4th edition. 1996 Williams & Wilkins.

Kessler DA, The End of Overeating: Taking Control of the Insatiable American Appetite. Rodale Books, 2010.

Kirk EP, Jacobsen DJ, Gibson C, Hill JO, Donnelly JED, Time course for changes in aerobic capacity and body composition in overweight men and women in response to long-term exercise: the Midwest Exercise Trial (MET).Int J Obes Relate Metab Disord. 2003 Aug;.27 (8): 912-9.

Kirschenbaum DS, The 9 Truths about Weight Loss: The No-Tricks, No-Nonsense Plan for Lifelong Weight Control. Henry Holt 2000, p 22.

Knechtle B, Knechtle P, Rosemann T, Skin-fold thickness and training volume in ultra-triathletes. Int J Sports Med 2009; 30: 343-347.

Kondor S, Aerodynamics. What is it worth to you? 6/09. www.TheSportfactory.com

Kovacs, Betty MD, RD. Alcohol and Nutrition. www.Medicinenet.com. (retrieved) 7/6/2009.

Kvist H, Hallgen P, Jonsson L, et al. Distribution of adipose tissue and muscle mass in alcoholic men. Metabolism, 1993, 42, 569-573.

Landers GJ, Blanksby BA, Ackland TR, Smith D. Morphology and performance of world championship triathletes. Ann Hum Biol. 2000 Jul-Aug;27(4):387-400.

Latner JD, Rosewall JK, Chisholm AM. Food volume effects on intake and appetite in women with binge-eating disorder and weight-matched controls. Int J Eat Disord. 2009 Jan; 42 (1): 68-75.

Le Carvennec M, Fagour C, Adenis-Lemarre E, Perlemoine C, Gin H, Regalleau V. Body composition of obese subjects by air displacement pelthysmography: The Influence of Hydration. Obesity, 2007

Lebenstedt M, Platte P, Pirke KM, Reduced resting metabolic rate in athletes with menstrual disorders. Med Sci Sports Exerc. 1999, 31(9): 1250-1256,

Lebenstedt M, Platte P, Pirke KM. Reduced resting metabolic rate in athletes with menstrual disorders. Med Sci Sports Exerc.1999 31(9): 1250-1256,

Lopez P, Ledoux M, Garrell DR. Increased thermogenic response to food and fat oxidation in female athletes: relationship with VO2 max. Am J Physiol Endocriol Metab. 2000 Sept; 279 (3): E601-7.

Loucks AB. Energy availability, not body fatness, regulates reproductive function in women. Exerc Sport Sci Rev. 2003;31:144-8

Lowensteyn I, Signorile JF, Giltz K, The Effect of Varying Body Composition on Swimming Performance, Journal of Strength and Conditioning Research, 1994 vol. 8 (3), 149-154.

MacLaren D, Reilly T, Lees A, Biomechanics and Medicine in VI, Taylor & Francis 1992.

Male and female young triathletes. J Sports Med Phys Fitness. 1996 Dec;36(4):265-70.

Malhotra, A. Noakes, T, Phinney, S. (2015). It is time to bust the myth of physical inactivity and obesity: you cannot outrun a bad diet Br J Sports Med doi:10.1136/bjsports-2015-094911

Mayo Clinic. http://www.mayoclinic.com/health/body-dysmorphic-disorder/DS00559 6/09

McClung M, Collins D. Because I know it will: placebo effects of an ergogenic aid on athletic performance. J Sport Exerc Psychol. 2007 Jun; 29 (3): 382-94.

McElroy M. Resistance to Exercise: A Social Analysis of Inactivity. 2002 Human Kinetics, p. 26.

McLean JA, Barr SI, Cognitive dietary restraint is associated with eating behaviors, lifestyle practices, personality characteristics and menstrual irregularity in college women. Appetite. 2003 40: 185-192.

Mennella, J. A. (2006). Development of food preferences: Lessons learned from longitudinal and experimental studies. Food Quality and Preference, 17(7-8), 635–637. http://doi.org/10.1016/j.foodqual.2006.01.008

Miller-Kovach K, Hermann M, Winick M. The psychological ramifications of weight management. J Womens Health Gend Based Med. 1999 May; 8 (4): 477-82.

National Eating Disorders Association. www.nationaleatingdisorders.org July 2009

National Weight Control Registry, www.nwcr.ws (retrieved August 2009)

National Weight Control Registry, www.nwcr.ws (retrieved July 2009)

Nicklas BJ, Wang X, You T, Lyles MF et al Effect of exercise intensity on abdominal fat lass during calorie restriction in overweight and obese post menopausal women: a randomized, controlled trial. Am J Clin Nutr. 2009 Apr; 89 (4): 104-52. Epub 2009 Feb 11.

Effect of Body fatness on tolerance to uncompensable heat stress. J Appl Physiol 2001 91: 2055-2063.

Otis CL, Drinkwater B, Johnson M, Loucks A, Wilmore J. American College of Sports Medicine position stand. The Female Athlete Triad. Med Sci Sports Exerc. 1997 May; 29 (5): i-ix. Comment in: Med Sci Sports Exerc. 1997 Dec; 29 (12): 1669-71.

Padilla S, Mujika I, Cuesta G, Goiriena JJ. Level ground and uphill cycling ability in professional road cycling. Med Sci Sports Exerc. 1999 Jun; 31 (6): 878-85.

Padilla S, Mujika I, Cuesta G, Polo JM, Chatard JC. Validity of a velodrome test for competitive road cyclists. Eur J Appl Physiol Occup Physiol. 1996; 73 (5): 446-51.

Pendergast DR, Di Prampero PE, Craig AB Jr, Wilson DR, Rennie DW.

Philips, KA. The Broken Mirror, Oxford University Press, 2005 ed.

Polivy J, Herman CP. Dieting and Binging: A causal analysis. American Psychologist 1985, 40: 193-201.

Puldem A, M.D., Lederman M, M.D. The Forks Over Knives Plan: How to Transition to the Life-Saving, Whole-Food, Plant-Based Diet by, Touchstone, 2014.

Quantitative analysis of the front crawl in men and women. J Appl Physiol. 1977 Sep; 43 (3): 475-9.

Raben A, Agerhlom-Larsen L, Flint A, Holst JJ, Astrup A. Meals with similar energy densities but rich in protein, fat , carbohydrate, or alcohol have different effects on energy expenditure and substrate metabolism but not on appetite and energy intake. American Journal of Clinical Nutrition, 2003, 77, 91-100.

Raynor HA, Jeffrey RW, Phelan S, Hill JO, Wing RR. Amount of food group variety consumed in the diet and long-term weight loss maintenance. 2005 Obes Res. 2005 May; 13 (5): 883-90.

Reed P. The Extra Mile. 2006 Rodale Books. p. 26.

Reynolds WW,. Karlotski WJ. The Allometric Relationship of Skeleton Weight to Body Weight in Teleost Fishes: A Preliminary Comparison with Birds and Mammals. 1977. Copeia: 160–163.

Rolls B. The relationship between dietary energy density and energy intake. J.Physiol Behav. 2009 Jul 14; 97 (5): 609-15. Epub 2009 Mar 20.

Ryan M. Sport Nutrition For Endurance Athletes. 2007 Velopress

Saulsbury CV. Power Hungry: The Ultimate Energy Bar Cookbook. Lake Isle Press, 2013.

Selkirk GA, McLellan TM. Influence of aerobic fitness and body fatness on tolerance to uncompensable heat stress. J Appl Physiol (1985). 2001 Nov; 91 (5): 2055-63.

Shephard and Astrand. Endurance In Sport,(1992) Blackwell Scientific Publications, p. 254.

Sleivert GG, Rowlands DS, Physical and physiological factors associated with success in the triathlon. Sports Med. 1996 Jul; 22 (1): 8-18.

Soenen S, Westerterp-Plantenga MS. Proteins and satiety: implications for weight management. Curr Opin Clin Nutr Metab Care. 2008 Nov; 11 (6): 747-51.

Sorrento RM, HigginsET. Handbook of motivation and cognition, Vol 2: Foundations of social behaviour. Guilford Press 1990. p. 135-136.

Stiegler P, Cunliffe A. The role of diet and exercise for the maintenance of fat-free mass and resting metabolic rate during weight loss. Sports Med. 2006; 36 (3): 239-62.

Stroud M. The Nutritional demands of very prolonged exercise in man. Proceedings of the Nutrition Society 1998, 57, 55-61.

Swan PD, McConnell KE. Anthropometry and bioelectrical impedance inconsistently predicts fatness in women with regional adiposity. Med Sci Sports Exerc. 1999 Jul; 31 (7): 1068-75.

Tanake M, Itoh K, Abe S, et al. Irregular patterns in the daily weight chart at night predict body weight regain. Exper Bio and Med 2004 229: 940-945.

Tardie, Gregory (2008). Glycogen Replenishment After Exhaustive Exercise. By U.S. Sports Academy in Sports Coaching, Sports Exercise Science, Sports Studies and Sports Psychology.

Teixeira PJ, Going SB, Houtkooper LB, Cussler EC, Blew RM, Sardinha LB , et al. Exercise motivation, eating, and body image variables as predictors of weight control. 2006 Med Sci Sports Exerc vol 38, 1: 179-188.

Thomas B, Lim A. Feed Zone Portables: A Cookbook of On-the-Go Food for Athletes. Velo Press, 2013.

United States Olympic Committee website. (retrieved 3/2009)

Van Loan, MD, Keim NL, Barbieri, TF & Mayclin, PL. The effects of endurance exercise with and without a reduction of energy intake on fat-free mass and the composition of fat-free mass in obese women. European Journal of Clinical Nutrition. 48 (6): 408-15, 1994

Van Weir MF, Ariens GA, Dekkers JC, Hendriksen IJ, Smid T, van Mechelen W. Phone and e-mail counseling are effective for weight management in an overweight working population: a randomized controlled trial. BMC Public Health 2009 Jan 9; (9): 6.

Varady KA, Santosa S, Jones PJ. Validation of hand-held bioelectrical impedance analysis with magnetic resonance imaging for the assessment of body composition in overweight women. American journal of human biology : the official journal of the Human Biology Council 2007; 19 (3): 429-33.

Varady KA, Santosa S, Jones PJ. Validation of hand-held bioelectrical impedance analysis with magnetic resonance imaging for the assessment of body composition in overweight women. Am J Hum Biol. 2007 May-Jun; 19; 3: 429-33.

Virnig AG, McLeod CR. Attitudes toward eating and exercise: A comparison of runners and triathletes. Journal of Sport Behavior. 1996 19, 82-90.

Wadstrom C, Backman L, Forsberg AM, Nilsson E, Hultman E, Reiszenstein P, Ekman M. Body composition and muscle constituents during weight loss: studies in obese patients following gastroplasty. June 2000, Obesity Surgery 10(3); 203-213.

Webb, Denise. (2014). Farewell to the 3,500-Calorie Rule Today's Dietitian Vol. 26, No. 11, p. 36.

Westerterp-Plantenga MS, Nieuwenhuizen A, Tome D, Soenen S, Westerterp KR. Dietary protein, weight loss, and weight maintenance. Annu Rev Nutr. 2009; (29): 21-41.

White P, Young K, Gillett J. Bodywork as a moral imperative: Some critical notes on health and fitness. Society and Leisure 1995, 18: 159-182.

Why alcohol calories are more important than you think. www.thefactsaboutfitness.com (retrieved July 2009)

Williams J. Shape up with the Slow fat Triathlete. 2009, Da Capo Press.

Wilson RS, James RS. Constraints on muscular performance: trade-offs between power output and fatigue resistance. Proc Biol Sci. 2004 May 7; 271 Suppl. 4: S222-5.

Wing RR, Phelan S. Long-term weight loss maintenance. Am J Clin Nutr 2005; (82) (suppl): 222s-5s.

Yang MU, Van Itallie TB. Composition of weight lost during short-term weight reduction. Metabolic responses of obese subjects to starvation and low-calorie ketogenic and nonketogenic diets. J Clin Invest. 1976 Sep; 58 (3): 722-30.

Yue G, Cole KJ. Strength increases from the motor program-comparison of training with maximal voluntary and imagined muscle contractions. J Neurophysiol 1992; 67 (5): 1114-23.

Footnotes

1   See Power Hungry: The Ultimate Energy Bar Cookbook by Camilla V. Saulsbury (Lake Isle Press, 2013) and Feed Zone Portables: A Cookbook of On-the-Go Food for Athletes by Biju Thomas and Allen Lim (Velo Press, 2013).

CREDITS

Cover design: Eva Feldmann

Layout and Typesetting: Sannah Inderelst

Photographs: Ingrid Loos Miller

                               ©Thinkstock

Copyediting: Elizabeth Evans, Manuel Morschel

ALL ABOUT TRIATHLON

384 p., in color, 133 Halftones

paperback,

16,5 x 24 cm

ISBN: 9781782550853

$ 24.95 US/$ 35.95 AUS

£ 16.95 UK/€ 22.95

Mark Kleanthous

THE COMPLETE BOOK OF TRIATHLON

The Complete Book of Triathlon is for all athletes who want to improve in or convert to the fascinating sport of triathlon. It shows among other things how to construct a training program, how to approach a competition and offers an Encyclopedia that covers all aspects of triathlon.

This book shows the triathlete and aspiring triathlete everything they need to know about triathlon, whether a sporting novice or an accomplished athlete in another sport. It tells you how to get started, what equipment to buy, the diet you will need, how to devise a training routine and how to arrange your busy life in order to accommodate it, and then explains how to finish a race, as well as how to recover from it. The Complete Book of Triathlon will tell you how to be the best that you can be in triathlon; not necessarily by training harder, but by training smarter.

All information subject to change © Thinkstock/Didgital Vision/Roger Weber

MEYER & MEYER SPORT

MEYER & MEYER
Sport
Von-Coels-Str. 390
52080 Aachen
Germany

Phone   +49 02 41 - 9 58 10 - 13
Fax   +49 02 41 - 9 58 10 - 10
E-Mail   sales@m-m-sports.com
Website   www.m-m-sports.com

All books available as E-books.

YOUR GUIDE FOR
LONG-DISTANCE TRAINING

Paul Huddle, Roch Frey
START TO FINISH

Okay, you've finished your first short-distance triathlon, maybe even an Olympic distance or half-distance triathlon. Now it's time to up the ante and go further and faster. Paul Huddle and Roch Frey are up to the challenge. Longer workouts, balancing work, family, and training, adding speed work, recovery, and the mental game are all essential when you decide to move up to the long distance.

No one has more training or racing experience than Roch and Paul. They will get you to your target race healthy, happy, and ready for more. Guaranteed.

The 24-week training program is laid out in four six-week increments. This represents the day-by-day, week-by-week work to be done in preparing for a successful long-distance triathlon.

192 p., in color, 200 Halftones,

26 illus., paperback,

16,5 x 24 cm

ISBN: 9781782550860

$ 19.95 US/$ 29.95 AUS

£ 12.95 UK/€ 18.95

MEYER
& MEYER
SPORT